About the author

Trevor Averre-Beeso attended Sunbury (_____ ___ obtained a BSc in economics at the University of Bradford and a DipEd at the University of Leeds. Within a few years of qualifying, Trevor attained a head of year position at The Boswells School, quickly progressing to become head of the school's sixth-form college in 1988.

Trevor became the youngest secondary head teacher in the UK when he was appointed head of Mayfield School, Redbridge, London, aged just thirty-five. He held the post for seven years.

He moved to Islington Green School in 2002. Islington Green had a troubled past. Nine months after Trevor joined the school, it passed its inspection, and the registered inspector described Trevor as 'visionary and transformational' in communicating his effective vision to parents, teachers and students alike.

In 2007, Trevor was named one of the top 100 up-and-coming most influential people in London in an Evening Standard poll and became a Fellow of the Royal Society of Arts.

Trevor co-founded Lilac Sky Schools in 2009 and is today CEO of Lilac Sky Schools and the Lilac Sky Academy Trust. Lilac Sky has worked with over 200 schools.

Supporting Schools' Success

www.lilacskyschools.co.uk

|0| **ways to transform a school**

WE DON'T NEED NO EDUCATION

By
Trevor Averre-Beeson

PRESS

PG Press – PGP

Published by PG Press (PGP)

Mountain Farmhouse, Marden Road,
Marden, Kent TN12 9PZ
Telephone: +44 (0) 1622 831310
info@pgpress.co.uk
www.pgpress.co.uk

© Trevor Averre-Beeson 2014
Printed by

Berforts Group – Stevenage and Hastings
ISBN – 978-1-910563-00-7

For Victoria, Samantha,
Annie and little Archie

Acknowledgements

Thanks are due to Stanley Rolls, the inspiring economics teacher who encouraged me to become a teacher in the first place, and to Hugh Ritchie, who I don't think knows it but whose laconic, calm and intelligent advice has stayed with me since I worked with him in the early nineties.

I want to thank Cec Darker, the chair of governors at Islington Green School when I joined. She took a chance on me and stayed the course as a mentor and friend. Without that leap in the dark, I would not have experienced much that I have since.

Also thanks to Jane Fielding, my business and life partner for the past ten years. She has had most of my good ideas during that period and has a natural flair for pushing me to take enterprising risks. And, of course, she gave birth to our beautiful son, Archie.

I am also grateful to Chris Bowler, my old sparring partner from deputy head days. He has remained a loyal and reliable friend and business partner for over twenty years.

I must also thank Peter Hyman, the author and former speech writer who worked for ten years with Tony Blair when he was Prime Minister. Peter introduced me to a wider political and educational world and encouraged me to develop my leadership strategy when he joined me at Islington Green. I learned a lot from him and owe him a debt.

Janus Van Helftern has also been a constant source of advice and encouragement.

Thanks too to my former Islington Green colleagues who still work for me now, Angela Gartland, Emma Catt, Marek Ostaszeweski, Jane Fielding and Jill Howson. They have been loyal advisers and team players and have also offered some feedback on the veracity of the stories contained in this book.

I also owe a debt of gratitude to all the staff and students at Islington Green School during my tenure. I learned a lot from everybody there and had the best of times. It was exciting, funny and hard work. It was probably the most challenging period of my life so far but it has stuck with me ever since. In particular I am grateful to Rachel Anderson, Karen Becker, John Challenor, Sherri Davis, Nick Hampton, Mike Harpham, Pete Hillman, Ken Muller, Keith Murzello, Chloe Parker, Ted Reilly, Mandy Seeburn, Jason Simmons, Debbie Smith, Jess Ward, Kenny Wellington, Tracy Wilson, Gill Young, Nick Hampton and Carla Barber as well as to the school's governors and to colleagues from the local authority, the Department for Education and London Challenge.

I would especially like to mention the late Ann Neal, who was my PA during these years and died tragically, shortly after I left Islington Green and just prior to joining me in my new school. Ann was my eyes and ears, was fiercely loyal and had a devilish sense of humour.

I must also thank my current long-suffering team: Kate Cooper (née Newman), Kelly Haley, Hayley Piddlington, David Houghton and Sam Busch. They are a relentless bunch who work as a very tight unit around me.

Thanks also to Teena Lyons at PG Press for her confidence, patience and faith in my story, and to the team at PG for editing and designing the book. Also, for their help and feedback and for reading the book in its early stages, thanks go to my PA, Kate (also for diving into the TES archives with her mum); my daughter Vicky; and my brother, Martin.

Finally, I am grateful to my redoubtable mother, Audrey, for her longevity, support and love throughout the years of my life and in my profession and the writing of this book.

I want to acknowledge my parents. My father, Archibald Norman, who died 36 years ago but remains an inspirational figure in spirit. He served in the Second World War, was a teacher, journalist and author himself and dragged his entire young family to Africa in the sixties to work at the University of Lagos. He gave me my first typewriter which I still proudly display in my office today.

Contents

INTRODUCTION

When it comes to failing schools, pretty much everyone has an opinion. Whether people advocate ditching the entire educational structure to try a new one, parachuting in someone from a champion's league of 'super-heads' to sort out individual schools or forcing more parental engagement, it seems there are solutions coming from all sides. Many ideas are dismissed as political sound-bites and those solutions that are implemented never seem to stay the course.

I've never said I hold all the answers, but I like to think I know more than most, mainly because I have had practical experience as the head of several failing schools. The media have dubbed people like me 'super-heads' because we are the ones who are sent in to sort out the schools that appear to be in a never-ending downwards spiral. In my view, though, there is no need for the 'super' epithet because much of what we do is plain common sense. There is no magic or sleight of hand required. What is needed is to take control of the issues, recognise the limitations of what we all have to work with and get on with the job in a structured, orderly way.

I am probably best known for my time at the helm of Islington Green School during some of its most difficult years, between 2002 and 2008. Islington Green is an institution that is famous for two things. The first of those claims to fame occurred well before my time. Pupils from the school's fourth-form music class provided the backing track for the Pink Floyd 1979 hit 'Another Brick in the Wall', belting out the chorus 'We don't need no education' with confidence and conviction. In typically rock-'n'-roll style, the music teacher Alun Renshaw took the young teens out of lessons to nearby Britannia Row Studios without the head Margaret Maden's permission. The Inner London Education Authority described this as 'scandalous' and Maden was so incensed she banned the children from appearing on *Top of the Pops* or in the music video. The fierce reactions were wholly typical of the divisions that characterised the school though subsequent years. Islington Green stubbornly held on to its 'them and us' culture and, even years on, successive generations of pupils continued to regularly chant the anthem's rallying cry in the school corridors.

The second significant event in Islington Green's history came in 1995 when overnight it became known as 'the school snubbed by Tony Blair' after the then opposition leader chose to send his son out of the borough and to another school across the capital even though he lived just a few doors away. This was the beginning of an especially dark time for Islington Green, which was subsequently placed into special measures on the day the Labour Party swept to victory two years later. Confidence among the staff plummeted. Many teachers were convinced they were the victims of a conspiracy cooked up by the newly elected Labour government to justify their leader's earlier decision. Dozens of good teachers headed for the exits and the already poor results at the school went into free-fall. Hardly surprisingly, pupils believed they went to a rubbish school because everyone kept telling them just that. Pretty soon this became a self-fulfilling prophecy.

After that, the school never seemed to be out of the media spotlight. Everything that happened either in or around Islington Green was scrutinised and picked over by the press. Commentators were apparently ever eager to prove, disprove, argue over or analyse Blair's decision. The story just wouldn't go away. In the months before I joined, for example, there was a high-profile court case involving one teacher suing for unfair dismissal over allegations of assault by pupils while she was pregnant. It was a serious subject but it is unlikely such a story elsewhere would have made it onto mainstream TV news programmes.

I couldn't help, therefore, but be acutely aware of the school's background before I took the job. Eager to get a rounded viewpoint, I did my own homework and found there was a surprisingly strong will in the community to turn things around. The school certainly wasn't seen as the lost cause some people were eager to portray it as. I also found that the school was staffed with a number of dynamic teachers, despite the flood of defections following the Ofsted blow. The few that had stayed were determined to prove everyone wrong. I had an overwhelming impression that the school had lost its way and simply needed direction.

Islington Green was my second headship. My approach there, and indeed in the schools I have led since, evolved over the years. In the early days, before I became a head teacher, I developed my leadership style through the time-honoured fashion of observing how others did it wrong and resolving that a different approach might be more effective. Then, later on, when I got my first headship at Mayfield School, in Redbridge, London, at the age of thirty-five, I was able to put my more ambitious plans into practice. I have also been extremely fortunate that, along the way, I have worked with some wise and highly inspirational people. Hugh Richie, the head at Alec Hunter when I was deputy there, was then and continues to be an inspirational role model. Chris Bowler, who was a deputy alongside me at Alec Hunter, has also been a constant and steady sounding board.

Another important, although perhaps unlikely, ally (considering the role of his former boss) was Tony Blair's one-time speechwriter Peter Hyman. Peter joined me part way through my headship at Islington Green and worked alongside me during the most turbulent years leading up to the school's switch to academy status.

Peter wrote a book about his experiences, *1 out of 10: From Downing Street Vision to Classroom Reality*, that documents a great deal about what was happening at Islington Green at that time, along with providing some astute and informed political commentary. While I very much enjoyed his take on what we did, I still feel there is room to explore it further in the context of how our experience there can be used to help other failing schools today.

During my near-five-year watch, Islington Green passed its inspection, came out of special measures and was described as 'good'. It also doubled its exam success, reduced exclusions from a high of 410 to low single figures and became fully staffed, popular and over-subscribed. During this time I was flattered to be described as a 'visionary leader' by inspectors.

It wasn't a one-off either. I have used many of the ideas implemented at Islington Green at other UK schools with similar success rates. Since leaving Islington Green, I have continued to develop, refine and use what I learned there and previously, firstly as a consultant head and then in my present job as founder and chief executive at Lilac Sky Schools. Lilac Sky Schools has worked with more than 200 schools and, at the time of writing, runs over sixteen schools in a mixture of Lilac Sky Trust academies and schools run on behalf of local authorities.

We Don't Need No Education is a book about leadership and how it is possible to change our schools for the better with a little thought and application and a great deal of positivity. I have explained my ideas through the story of my time at Islington Green, partly because it is the most intense and amplified example of a turnaround in my career. I also believe that, following the acres of coverage of that time, it is time to set the record straight on a few of the conspiracy theories that dominated that period.

The techniques and ideas outlined here would, however,

be effective at any school, failing or otherwise, and have already been proven to get results time and again.

I have never wavered from my early view that running a school successfully, however challenging the conditions, is not rocket science and that no super-human powers are required. What is needed is effective leadership in order for heads to foster good relations with all stakeholders, from parents and the community to teachers and pupils, and an effective system of rewards and motivation.

Time and again I have visited failing schools and found head teachers hiding. They either physically hide, by literally not allowing parents, children or teachers anywhere near them, or metaphorically hide behind a fiendish system of punishments and exclusions that means they never truly have to come face to face with the real issues. Not surprisingly, neither approach is particularly effective. Hiding just means everyone around a school becomes increasingly frustrated and even small problems just keep on getting bigger. And the already big problems go off scale. Those heads who resort to ramping up the punishments ironically induce just the effect they hope to see off. Behaviour will actually get worse. Why? If behaviour rules are ever to work properly, there needs to be a balanced approach. Children need to know they will be punished if they break the rules but rewarded, or at least noticed, when they do something right. There is absolutely no place in our schools for knee-jerk punishments to ensure good behaviour. We should all be focussing our energies on looking at ways to promote a positive atmosphere in the classroom.

Introduction

One of the most common mistakes I see in troubled schools is a lack of consistency. This is not a big surprise because it is not in human nature to be consistent or relentless. However, before anything can really change, the head has to get to grips with this inconsistency. Without clear rules and patterns of behaviour, chaos will always follow. When teachers individually devise their own rules and sanctions, it is no wonder children get confused. One teacher may make a big thing about insisting on raised hands while another might not want them. One may demand silence while another positively encourages children to talk. If pupils see a lack of consistency among the people heading the classroom, is it any wonder they make up their own rules?

My philosophy on turning around schools centres on improving behaviour management because, if you get children to be calm and concentrate, good results will naturally follow. This is not complicated either. Indeed, it can be achieved in three easy steps. The number-one rule is to be constantly positive, because you always get back what you give out. Secondly, it is up to the adults to set the controls. They have that right and should exercise it. Thirdly, we all need to be relentless. Giving up too soon is what really lets down our schools.

After my time working in challenging schools I am utterly convinced of one thing in particular: it is possible to get even the most difficult children to behave. With enough will and determination, we can all learn how to achieve this. We owe it to the children of this generation and the next to try.

Action is still urgently required, too. According to official Ofsted statistics, 1.5 million children are being educated in weak schools.[1] Although there has been a 9 per cent rise in schools being rated as good or outstanding, there are still an embarrassing number of children who attend schools that are considered to be underperforming. It is too easy to put the blame on a lack of funding, and this is a problem. However, it is not the only issue. The fact is, there are cracks in the foundations and, until many other issues are addressed, no amount of extra cash will solve the underlying issues.

Ongoing training and development for teachers are, for example, woefully inadequate. Making any significant changes to a school relies on effective teaching and it is for this reason that I have always believed in working closely with my team. I am a strong believer in setting clear learning objectives and putting in place effective training programmes for the long-term development of teachers.

Schools have not got to grips with coaching their staff and refreshing their learning to keep up with the latest techniques. Training programmes are, of course, down to heads in individual schools, but, perhaps unsurprisingly, they fall a long way down the 'to do' list in failing schools. Heads in these situations assume, rightly or wrongly, that introducing a training programme will be seen as an adversarial move. The thinking goes that it shifts the focus onto teachers and implies they are failing. Training

---

1. Ofsted, September 2013, www.ofsted.gov.uk.

courses are viewed from a highly critical, even hostile, angle. This does not mean they should be abandoned, though. In my view, we should be working on ways to understand and promote the importance of ongoing training because it will make a huge difference.

Another aspect of schooling that urgently needs to be addressed is the issue of governance. At the time of writing, governance has been much in the news following the so-called Trojan Horse scandal in Birmingham and an alleged Islamic plot to exert a dominant influence over schools in the city. This story has highlighted wider issues about governance too. We need to urgently review the experience and qualifications of groups that have a large influence over our schools and also the way in which they operate. In recent years, we have fallen into a style of governorship not dissimilar to the one we see used in the football league. Governors appoint heads and tell them they are in charge and should get on with it and do what needs to be done. Two years on, under pressure for results, the governors pop up and say they are not sure whether things are going quite as they hoped and the head is the problem. Then, in the same way as football managers are hoiked out mid-season after a run of bad scores, heads are rapidly replaced. No one can perform effectively under a regime like this. It simply pushes the focus onto short-term 'crowd-pleasing' results and does little for the long-term success of a school, which is what is needed to sustain it year after year.

One of the biggest problems we face is that people are unwilling to properly discuss issues such as governance and training. Indeed, there is a sense of helplessness running as an undercurrent to any discussion about schools today. People will say with a shrug that the real problem is that kids today are less respectful of adults, teachers and society. They are more violent and streetwise and they roam in gangs terrorising teachers and local residents alike. They are not as academic or prepared for the world of work. In short, it is that old cliché: kids today aren't what they used to be. That is the issue.

This view is far too simplistic. It is wrong on many levels, but mostly because it reduces education to a black-and-white issue in which there are winners and losers, goodies and baddies. My experience of media scrutiny at Islington Green, and indeed before my time there, showed me the press needs two opposing sides and is not too bothered by the nuances of the argument. This needs to change if we want to move forward.

In recent times, for example, teachers have had a very unsympathetic airing thanks to a series of strikes. Watching the coverage, I was surprised by how little was made of the reasons for them withdrawing their labour. I do believe they should be given a fair hearing, but on all the evidence there is very little chance of that.

This is not to say all teachers are perfect. Indeed, for all my personal experience in schools, this point was brought home to me most sharply when I watched one of the many recent reality TV outpourings in the field, with shows such as *Educating Essex and Educating Yorkshire*. One episode that had me reaching for the off switch showed an extraordinary confrontation between a deputy head and a fifteen-year-old girl.

The girl, let's call her Aisha, had arrived at school wearing a hat in clear contravention of the rules on uniform. She'd barely got through the door before she was confronted by the deputy head, who ordered her to take it off. There was obviously some history between the two, because Aisha didn't just refuse to remove the hat; she also gave the man a mouthful that colourfully outlined her frustration at his almost constant criticism. His reaction? With much finger wagging, he declared he would follow Aisha around the school until she removed the offending headgear.

'I'm going to follow you,' he stormed. 'I'm going to follow you and follow you. I will follow you to the grave.'

And he did. The cameras greedily pursued the story as the deputy trailed Aisha around the school. As he did, he kept up a barrage of questions along the lines of how many times he had told her, why did she think she could ignore him and so on. Eventually, the girl could take no more and after the deputy literally backed her into a corner she physically and verbally lashed out.

Not surprisingly, the story created banner headlines. It was a gift to tabloid papers and reinforced many already deeply held prejudices about the state of our schools. In all the rhetoric that followed, no one seemed to ask the very obvious question, which was: what on earth was this teacher doing? He was the adult, in a position of responsibility, yet he was behaving like a playground bully.

Episodes like this do nothing to reduce inbuilt prejudices about our schools, and my experience shows there is little that can be done to stop the media pursuing these views. However, this is not to say we can't transform our schools from within, provoke a wider, more considered debate and alter the argument by proving the detractors wrong.

One of the best bits of advice I ever got came when I was a deputy at Alec Hunter in Essex. Headmaster Hugh Ritchie took me to one side and said: 'If you think there is a problem, do something. If you don't deal with it, it will remain a problem and will probably become a bigger problem.'

He was right. While it is prudent to let some niggly things pass, this doesn't give anyone carte blanche to ignore all problems, which is what I fear is happening today in our schools. Problem solving is, after all, the essence of what head teachers should be doing and the best way to solve any problem is to tackle it head on.

It is not always easy to make the right decision and the ones you do make won't always please everyone. That doesn't mean you should shy away from acting, though. One of the hardest parts of leading schools is that everyone has a view on what needs to be done and no one is afraid to voice it. This was particularly the case at Islington Green, where I was under almost constant pressure from all sides, both internally and externally.

Introduction

The job of a head teacher is to be the person who makes the sensible decisions in the face of all countervailing pressures. Whether it is the staff toilet being broken, the union kicking off, parents complaining or the local authority telling you what to do, you still have to do the right thing. Anyone who makes a decision to appease some factional pressure from another group is on a hiding to nothing. What they should be doing is standing up and saying, 'I understand all that, but what we need to do here is the very best job for the children. I know others may lose a little bit in terms of time or money, but we need to do it.' That is leadership.

It is not good enough to opt out by shaking our heads and saying that kids today aren't what they used to be. That's just an excuse. In fact, as Sheila, the deputy at Mayfield, my first London school, once memorably told me, 'Kids are just kids.' She was right. I had previously been told by an Essex colleague that working in a London school was 'heart-attack country', but Sheila's assessment was in fact far more accurate. Despite the huge cultural, political and economic mix of families I have worked with, kids are only ever, well, still kids. They may be white, black or Asian, middle class or working class, destined to become company directors or taxi drivers, but they behave the same in schools wherever you go. It makes no sense to treat them differently.

While at Mayfield, I had a very clear demonstration of this. Mr Jones, a local resident whose outer wall faced the alleyway that the students walked down on their way home, approached me. He was distressed about the children hanging around, drinking, smoking and fighting but what really upset him was the amount of graffiti on his wall. There was so much of it, it was impossible to see the white wall underneath. He told me he painted his wall every two years but the graffiti always returned.

My first thought was that, if you give children a blank canvas in a secluded spot, they will probably always write on it. However, I agreed to look into it and sent Sheila down to the offending wall to identify as many names as we could of students who had been expressing their creativity there. We rounded up the ten culprits and I gave them a lecture on the impact they can have on strangers through unthinking actions. I also sent the school caretakers to the alleyway to clear it of weeds and bought some black paint. I figured the wall was practically black anyhow, through the indelible marker used for the graffiti, so we might as well go all the way. It would make it hard for the children to start their artwork again.

The wall remained graffiti free for the whole of the rest of the time I was at the school. Mr Jones saw me some time later and said he thought it was a miracle. He had been telling all his neighbours, friends and family what we'd done. 'It's amazing how much the kids have changed,' he said.

What struck me most about this incident was how resigned Mr Jones had been to the behaviours he was seeing. Even though he was an adult, he had given up on his ability to influence children. A simple nudge changed all that. The kids didn't change, though. The adults did.

Children behave in the way adults let them and the real issue is that adults have lost track of their part in all of this. The way we run schools and behave as adults has a lot to do with the way children respond. Indeed, instead of focussing our energies on discussing the trouble with kids today, perhaps it is time to look more closely at the trouble with adults today. We all – parents, teachers, authorities and head teachers – have a part to play in our children's upbringing. We owe it to them to up our game.

Chapter One

COOL RECEPTION

When Islington Green School offered me the headship in 2002, the decision on whether to take it was not easy. While the £100,000 salary on offer was pretty compelling, indeed more than double what I was then on as the head of Mayfield School, the reason the figure was so high was because the position was not one that many people wanted to take on. It was very obvious, even in the brief time I had spent at the school during the interview process, that turning Islington Green around was a very big job indeed.

Everybody had a view about Islington Green. It is the inner-city comprehensive famously rejected by Tony Blair, who chose to send his son Euan across London to the grant-maintained Catholic London Oratory. Then, to add insult to injury, in May 1997, just as the UK was waking up to the news of the Labour election landside, it emerged that Islington Green had been placed in special measures.

Teachers and unions immediately cried foul. They tried desperately to cast light on the exceptional timing that appeared to vindicate the new Prime Minister's decision. Yes, they said, the school had problems, but it was not failing. Morale was apparently good and GCSE results were respectable, with 38 per cent getting five A*s to Cs. No one could believe the outcome of the Ofsted inspection. Indeed, on the day that the then head Tony Garwood called the staff together to tell them about the failed inspection, National Union of Teachers (NUT) rep Ken Muller had arrived at the school clutching a bottle of champagne for the dual celebration of Labour's victory and the expected successful Ofsted results.

In the months that followed, the school pretty much imploded, according to people who were there at the time. Morale plummeted and many parents pulled their kids out of the school. Those children who were left behind probably couldn't help but make the connection that, since they went to a failing school, they themselves were probably not worth bothering with because they were destined for the scrap heap. Tony Garwood, under pressure to make visible changes, discarded mixed-ability teaching, leading to a wave of resignations. Indeed, within two years almost all the teachers there in 1997 had gone.

It was a far cry from the school's heyday just five years earlier, when Christine Peters, a popular and progressive head teacher, had made great inroads to turn the school around. Although the site was not ideal (the school building was a 1960s seven-storey tower block and the catchment area was dominated by social housing), Peters had begun to attract some of the more affluent families in the area. However, some observers believed the school was in some way a victim of its own success. By the mid-nineties, it had risen to become the school with the second-best GCSE results in the borough, which attracted more local parents and squeezed out the professionals from further afield. Arguably, the school didn't respond fast enough to the challenges of the changing intake; however, all that was academic by the time the Ofsted verdict was delivered. After that, the downfall accelerated at a dizzying rate. In a short space of time, GCSE results at Islington Green dropped to below 25 per cent A*s to Cs.

In the autumn of 2001, when I spotted the job was being advertised, the school had been through three more heads and nine further Ofsted inspections. It was out of special measures by the year 2000 but it was still rated as having serious weaknesses. Exclusions were running at a record high, with 410 in the previous twelve months, and GCSE results had sunk to a new low of 11 per cent A*s to Cs. There was still a huge job to be done and the incumbent head, Marion Parsons, was quite open about her reasons for quitting: she didn't have the stamina to turn the school around.

I had just spent the past seven years on a project to turn around Mayfield School in east London. Ofsted didn't categorise schools so specifically back then, but when I joined in 1996 Mayfield had just had an inspection and the headline of the report was that the school had serious weaknesses, including poor behaviour, question marks over the quality of teaching, bad exam results and far too many exclusions. The experience had been a bit of a baptism by fire, but it occurred to me that Islington Green suffered from many of the same problems as Mayfield, albeit on a larger scale. I had managed to turn Mayfield around from 20 per cent five A*s to Cs to 47 per cent and the school was running pretty smoothly. Indeed, I found myself coming in one morning and wondering what I should do next. That was the moment I knew that I had to move on and try something else.

Funnily enough, at around that time, I got a call to see whether I would like to go to another Islington school: Highbury Grove. I went to take a look but quickly decided it wasn't for me. Then I saw the ad for the Islington Green job. That got my attention.

From a personal point of view, there was the very inviting prospect that I would get my hands on the platinum discs of Pink Floyd's 'Another Brick in the Wall', which had played its part in making the school so famous, or should that be infamous. Islington Green pupils had sung the now anthem-like chorus 'we don't need no education' in Pink Floyd's 1979 hit song. As a teenager I had been massively into the music scene, both playing guitar and composing songs. My group The Press was even signed to the EMI label for a brief, heady period while I was at university. Sadly my dreams of pop stardom came to naught, although I can claim to have been the support act for a number of well-known groups including the Pretenders and the Rolling Stones. You might say music ran in my blood, but at the very least I felt that I understood the magic of those two platinum discs a lot more than most.

When I went for my interview I spotted them on the wall behind the head's desk, although it immediately irritated me that they had been placed in a position that was so high up. I had to crane my neck to see them and promised myself then and there that, if I got the job, they'd be straight down and placed in pride of place behind my desk at eye level.

I'd be lying, though, if I didn't say it was the salary that swung it. The discs were great and had lovely nostalgic value, but I found my first few hours at Islington Green a shocking experience. It was unlike any school I had ever visited in my life.

The school itself is just off the bustling, chic shopping area of Upper Street. It was a shabby and uninviting concrete and glass monolith built on a tiny plot and skirted by high barbed-wire fences. It was surrounded on three sides by town houses that must have been worth at least a million pounds each. On the fourth side there was one of the most notorious housing estates in London. Back then, the estate housed members of the most well-known crime gangs in the capital. I'm not talking about kids larking around with the odd caper. These were grown men who were robbing, selling drugs and running protection rackets.

Getting into the school was chaos. The building had

just one entrance, which took you through an airlock and straight into the staff area. The governors, in their wisdom, had invited me in for an interview first thing on a Monday morning, at just the same time that 1,050 kids were jostling their way through the single door. No one took any notice of me as I stood and watched the kids swearing and shoving one another. At least 200 kids pushed past before I could find a gap in the human sea and jostle my way into the first part of the airlock. I spotted that up ahead the entrance divided into two, with one part intended for visitors and the other for children. Many of the kids were seizing the opportunity to squeeze into the visitors' line, to avoid the harassed senior member of staff who was shouting hopelessly about various dress-code infringements.

'Jimmy, Jimmy, you know you are not allowed to wear caps,' the teacher said, neatly reaching out and hooking the offending article off the child's head. 'Come and see me at the end of the day if you want it back.'

'Aw fucking hell sir, that's mine. My dad will go nuts.'

'You know the rules. Move along.'

Glancing to my left I saw a small square hole in the wall, rather like one of those butler hatches you get in old-fashioned kitchens. Tucked away in the cubbyhole was a woman who was clearly the receptionist. She looked utterly terrified and probably with good cause. She was surrounded by a group of angry teenagers demanding the return of various bits of confiscated property.

'You have my phone. Give it back to me, or I'll get my dad in here…'

It took some minutes before I could find anyone to announce that I had arrived, and eventually I was led down the graffiti-strewn corridor into Marion Parsons' office. Marion was what can only be described as a 'character'. She was hyperactive and slightly chaotic and had an alarming habit of calling everyone 'darling'. She'd come to Islington Green from a girls' grammar school. I suspected the hope had been that she'd be able to sprinkle some high-achieving magic on Islington Green, but she hadn't been able to lift it out of category.

Marion's office was huge and strewn with paper. What alarmed me most were the five entrances to the office, which both staff and children used freely as a cut-through. We were talking away about the job and people would just amble through. Marion was clearly so used to this that she didn't even acknowledge any of the trespassers and carried on blithely as though nothing had happened. Occasionally a student would burst in shouting, so the head couldn't ignore them.

'Miss, miss, when am I gonna get my cap back?' a girl yelled, with no self-consciousness about the fact the head was clearly engaged with a visitor.

I followed Marion's line of sight and saw a large postbag bulging with baseball caps.

'End of term, darling, end of term.'

'If you think I'm going to wait for the end of fucking term, you've got another thing coming.'

'No, come along, Sian. If you swear another time I will have to exclude you.'

'I don't fucking care.'

'That's it, Sian, you are excluded.'

I could hardly believe it. This place was mad. It was virtually ungovernable. Nothing worked and there seemed to be no thought whatsoever about how to make it work. The way people marched in and out of Marion's office was symptomatic of how out of control Islington Green had become.

I made a mental note that, if I got the job and agreed to take it, four of those five doors would go. There would be one entrance in and out and a person sat on the outside who would be charged with making sure that no one simply wandered in at will.

After we'd talked for about an hour, Marion decided to introduce me to the staff. Still talking non-stop, only breaking off to yell at a child about some dress-code infringement or another, she led me to a large L-shaped room on the first floor. It was clearly two rooms knocked together and was dirty, scruffy and filled with mismatched, stained and torn furniture. Lining one wall were around a dozen photocopiers from various eras, each with paper piled chaotically on every surface. There must have been more than 100 people in the room and my first thought was, where are the teachers? This lot wouldn't have looked out of place in a sixth-form common room. They were dressed scruffily in jeans and seemed to have an alarming air of indifference concerning the entrance of their current head. Looking around the group, I sensed tension in the air. It felt like they were all waiting for something and were completely resigned to the fact that what they were waiting for was going to be bad when it happened.

After a day at Islington Green I could hardly wait to get back to the sanctuary of my office at Mayfield. Slumping into my chair, I felt physically and emotionally exhausted.

'You don't look good,' said my PA, Brenda Steele, as she brought me a cup of tea. Brenda was always a great sounding board and always happy to sit down, listen to my thoughts and then proffer her opinion. She was also super-efficient with her filing and unwaveringly loyal. In fact, she was everything a good PA should be.

'I don't feel it,' I agreed, before telling her the story of my experience.

Brenda listened, wide eyed. When I finished she said, 'Are you sure you want to do this?'

'No, I am not sure I want to do it at all,' I admitted. 'I don't have a single clue where to start.'

'Why don't you do what you always do? Write a list. You've already named at least twenty things you'd like to change, so write them down.'

She was right. I got out my notebook and began to write straight away. The ideas just flowed out:

Block off all the doors to the headmaster's office.

Get my PA outside the door on crowd control.

Block off the downstairs corridor so it is for adults only.

Create a new entrance for children, separate from the visitor one.

In a short space of time I had fifty-one items on my list. Looking down at the bullet points, I grimaced. None of this would be easy to do. It would be tough enough in an ordinary school, but it would be nigh on impossible to get these things done in an atmosphere like the one I had seen on my visit. Plus, time was not on my side. It had taken seven years to transform Mayfield School, but, as I was acutely aware, the pressure was on to turn Islington Green around in a much shorter time frame. Indeed, the governors had made it clear they wanted results in weeks, let alone months or even years.

Even though I knew it would be the greatest challenge of my career to date, I had one important factor on my side: I wanted to do it. Yes, I had seen the school in its worst possible light, but I could still see what it could be.

When the job offer was made, I said yes straight away.

Once I had made my choice and resigned from Mayfield, I wanted to get going at Islington Green as soon as possible. It occurred to me that there was little point keeping my long list of action points to myself. I needed to share them with my new senior leadership team (SLT) to get them on board and pulling in the same direction. Even though my start date was some weeks away, I opted to kick things off with a call to arms at a specially convened, one-off SLT conference. This way, when I did finally arrive at the school, we could all hit the ground running. I envisaged an intense yet uplifting conference at a hotel. I would run through the problems, discuss my action points and finish with a rallying cry before we all shared a nice dinner in the evening. Everyone on my new team would go away inspired and invigorated, delighted that they were part of something exceptional.

That's not what happened at all.

At first none of the Islington Green SLT would even accept the invitation to my conference. It made sense to me to run it over a weekend, yet, as I quickly discovered, there was no way my highly unionised Islington Green colleagues would ever contemplate giving up even a second of their Saturday or Sundays, let alone several hours. OK, I said, let's do it on a Friday, then. They didn't want to do that either. In fairness to them, they were very aware that, if they left the school to its own devices for a few hours, all hell would probably have broken loose. Right then things were running on a knife edge at Islington Green and the SLT was constantly fire fighting.

Eventually, after much discussion and persuasion, the SLT agreed to attend the conference at a nearby hotel in London from 3.30pm on a Friday afternoon. I told them I would outline my plans and buy them a meal and they could return to their families first thing on Saturday morning. When I say 'agree', that is quite a loose interpretation. One look around the thunderous and thoroughly disinterested faces of my new colleagues on the evening of the event told me that no one there was a willing participant.

Cool reception

This is going to be hard work, I thought to myself. It would be bad enough if one or two looked so fed up, but all of them? This was the toughest crowd I had ever faced.

I couldn't let myself be put off, so I launched into my usual well-worn routine. It was the one I'd always used at conferences when I wanted to lighten the mood.

'Why don't we start by all telling a funny story about ourselves?' I said.

Silence enveloped the room and the atmosphere felt tense and threatening. In the distance I could hear the busy hum of normal hotel life. Forcing myself to focus, despite my growing unease, I continued.

'OK, how about I start? I was speaking at a heads' conference the other day. I was in a big room, a lot bigger than this in fact, and I started by saying what I always do, which is, "Can you hear me at the back?" Then, someone who was sat at the back piped up and said, "I can, but I'm willing to move somewhere I can't."'

The hush that greeted the punch line was deafening. Seven pairs of eyes stared back at me, unblinking and unmoved. The expression on each face in the room was utterly blank. OK, my anecdote was never going to get them rolling in the aisles, but it wasn't that bad. It had always served me well as a good opener and usually got a laugh. Sometimes, people who know me and who have heard it before even shout back the rejoinder. Here, there wasn't even a titter.

My spirits sank still further as we went around the room and each member of the SLT made half-hearted attempts to introduce themselves. One of the last people to speak was John Challenor, one of the older, more experienced group members, who had been at Islington Green for many years and was now one of the Deputy heads. He was a popular figure among the staff and had been acting head at one stage.

'I have a funny story,' he said, fixing his eyes on me and giving me a steady look. 'I was working in a school. It was a tough school and it went into special measures. We had head after head after head and then they made me head and I enjoyed the job. Then, they decided they were going to get in this super-head. He asked me to come to a meeting on a Friday night.'

As he finished, each member of the SLT threw back their head and roared with laughter. Judging by the reaction, this joke at my expense was clearly the most amusing thing they had heard for weeks. The noise shattered the thick atmosphere of the room, but it still felt awkward and forced.

Waving my hand to get them to settle down, I said, 'I can see you are not exactly over-joyed to be here and, let me say, I couldn't be more unhappy than you now I have seen your faces. I had no idea this evening was going to be like this.

'I am not going to spend too much time talking this evening because it is obvious it is not going to work. However, I have brought this list of action points and I want you to know every item on that list is going to happen. This isn't a list to prioritise, have a discussion about or change, or even remove some things altogether. You can offer to add things to it and if I agree we will do it. If I don't, we won't. This school is my problem now and I own this problem because I am the head.

'Things have to change because otherwise this school is going to crash and burn if it hasn't done so already. I just want you to know about it so when you start there won't be any surprises.'

There were no questions. Everyone made it very obvious they just wanted to go to dinner and get the event over with. The atmosphere between us didn't get much better over our meal, although some of the staff cheered up a little once the alcohol started flowing. No one made any effort to speak to me and I went up to my room early, leaving them all to it.

Sitting alone in my room, I felt pretty depressed. The evening had been a fiasco. This was the first time I had met my senior team properly and they had basically told me to get lost. If I let them get away with it, I may as well not bother to take up the job.

The following morning, over coffee and croissants, I told the SLT how things were going to be.

I said: 'Last night, I showed you the list and I tried to lighten the mood with some funny stories. It hasn't gone quite as I planned. I have been thinking about it overnight and I am going to be honest: this has been a bit of a disaster.

'I have come from a school I have been heading for seven years where everyone was very positive about the changes taking place. That school wasn't like this school, but it was pretty bad and I do know how to get from where you are to where you need to be. That is only going to happen if you are on board, if we have courteous and polite relationships and if we all act like adults with a code of conduct for professional behaviour. Like it or not, you are stuck with me.

'I have said I will do this job and will do so. If you don't want to do it with me, that is not a problem. Between now and when I start, we can decide. I will meet each of you individually and will ask you if you are up for it or not. If you say you are up for it, great, you know how it is going to be. If you are not up for it, you can either step off the leadership team or go and find another school. I will support you and do whatever else needs to be done. If we work together, things can only get better.'

My speech was met with yet another stony silence, except this time it had the added ingredient of surprise on the faces of many of my colleagues. A few of them did their best to present poker faces, still utterly unwilling to give any ground.

In the days that followed I began to have serious misgivings about doing the job at all. Teams are so important and, like every leader, I would be reliant on my senior people to put my ideas into practice. I could have hundreds of great ideas on how to put things right, but, without people to back them and implement them, they would only ever be ideas. Right then, though, I couldn't be certain the team I had would do anything

I asked of them. After an agonising few days, I decided to withdraw my application. Islington Green's governors didn't take it too well and immediately cut off all contact. Luckily the team at Mayfield School reluctantly agreed I could stay on.

Once the decision was made, I couldn't get Islington Green out of my mind. I kept thinking about my plans and what I could have achieved. Every time the pang of regret became too great I would remind myself of that awful evening with the SLT.

Could they change, though, I wondered? I am a realist. I know there is no such thing as the perfect employee, let alone team of employees. It is quite rare to find someone who is fired up to work to their upmost capabilities every waking hour and motivated to do what it takes. Yet, these people seemed so demotivated and far away from this ideal that surely transforming Islington Green would be an impossible task.

The longer I thought about it, though, the more I realised I had made a terrible mistake. I realised I really wanted the job and, perhaps more importantly, truly believed I was the right person to lead the transformation of the school even with my somewhat unenthusiastic team. Taking a deep breath, I called Islington Green and told the governors I had changed my mind and was keen to take the position if they still wanted me. I was quite open about my reasons for wavering and said the attitude of the SLT had really left me surprised and taken aback.

Luckily, the team at Islington Green were pleased to

hear from me, but in a fantastic twist of irony I was asked to attend a second interview conducted by the governors and some members of the SLT. The self-same team that had sat stony faced through my introductory event and made me rethink everything would now be part of a panel that decided my fate.

Amazingly, despite our obvious differences, the second interview must have gone in my favour because I was offered my job back. However, I was left in no doubt that the team's feelings about me hadn't improved. The salary on offer for the job was lowered by £15,000.

'Oh, we over-promised before,' I was told airily. 'That is all we can pay now.'

I could have rolled over and taken it, because it was still an astonishingly good salary, but I wasn't about to do so. The task ahead of me was huge and, if the school valued me enough to expect me to deliver, they needed to keep their side of the bargain. If they wanted me to get everyone to pull together and succeed, they had to pay me the rate they had promised. After a bit of a stand-off, I agreed to the lower figure as a main salary with the promise of a £15,000 allowance if I hit certain pre-agreed targets.

Of course, agreeing terms was the easy part. Next I had to figure out how to inspire the team and get them to work with me to make the transformation happen. The reason I had changed my mind was that I fully believed in the prospects for Islington Green; now I had to convince the team to help me make it happen, one way or another.

Chapter two

WHAT DO YOU WANT TO GO THERE FOR?

Ask me what I value most in a team and the answer will always be the same: loyalty. Once I am sure that my staff are lined up behind me and backing me all the way, everything else will fall into place.

After my somewhat shaky beginning at the SLT conference, one of my first acts before my official start date at Islington Green was to interview each of the SLT individually. I had warned them on the morning of the conference they would have the opportunity to tell me whether or not they were on board with what I wanted to do. If they were, great. If they weren't, well, we would have to have a serious discussion about their future.

The first interview I did was with John Challenor, the deputy who had made the big joke about the idiot who asked him to a meeting on a Friday night. I approached the meeting with trepidation because he had already demonstrated he had the ear of the other members of the team, so his attitude was probably going to set the tone of the subsequent interviews. I have to admit, I was surprised by his opening gambit.

'We've all talked about it and agreed, the conference wasn't our finest hour together,' he said before I really had a chance to say anything. 'We know we are just going to have to work if we want things to change, and we do.

'I am retiring at the end of the next academic year, but until then I will give you my support and will do what you say. I will do whatever is necessary to see you in.'

'Thank you very much,' I said, recovering my composure. 'It is good of you to come out and say that.'

John went on to give a fair assessment of who he believed was up to the job and where he saw weakness in the team. He named Dan as one man in particular whom he believed could be very damaging indeed.

'If I was you, I would get him out as quickly as you can,' he advised.

Right then, I wasn't sure whether John was giving me an accurate assessment, but it had taken courage to be so open, so I decided to trust him. Aside from this, my first impressions of Dan had not been good and I already had my doubts about whether he would make the grade.

'What are you suggesting I do?' I said.

'I would find him a secondment,' John replied with a shrug.

'OK. Can you find him one before I start?'

'I can try,' he said.

What do you want to go there for?

I liked John. Now we'd had time to get to know one another, I could see why he was popular among the team and already sensed he would be solidly reliable and a great help to me. He was in his early sixties, tall and well built, with a shock of spiky grey hair. He had a bit of an anarchic air, a characteristic that would always go down well with both the teachers and pupils at Islington Green. His no-nonsense approach to fights among pupils was legendary. He'd literally step into the fray of flailing fists, grab each child in an uncompromising arm-lock and march them away.

John had been at Islington Green for more than twenty years, so his resigned air had a lot to do with the fact he had seen many people come and go who had promised the earth and not delivered. I couldn't really bear a grudge for his attitude when we first met, and I didn't.

Over the following weeks, John helped organise an excellent secondment for Dan, getting him on a scheme that trains senior teachers to work in difficult schools. Dan did well on the course and subsequently got a headship in a small school.

The two interviews that followed were not so clear cut. One of the things Marion, the previous head, was well known for was promoting the interests of women. She had built up an impressive portfolio of women with strong personalities on the SLT; however, some were clearly not qualified to be there. One, for example, was a teaching assistant with no experience of leadership whatsoever and I had to ask her to step down. A few of the others who were left behind were not about to let me off lightly. Unfortunately, some of these women were so focussed on fighting for themselves, they completely forgot about the purpose of the meeting, which was to discover whether they were loyal to me and to my vision of the school.

Two women, in particular, stood out: Emma Catt and Hannah Taylor. Emma was a fiercely trendy young blond Islingtonite who invariably wore jeans and the latest trainers accessorised with flowing scarves and bangles. She was well liked among the staff and had a way about her that really appealed to the kids too. It is that certain something that some teachers just have. They remain perfectly calm but their manner means even the naughtiest kids step into line. Emma was in a long-term relationship with Marek, the head of English, who was also a very snappy dresser and a steely eyed chap who had a great way of keeping the kids in check.

Hannah was far more understated and a lot harder to read. It was obvious she was very professional and ruthlessly ambitious, but I sensed her loyalty would be hard won. There was a distance about her and an unwillingness to engage in anything but the barest pleasantries.

Both Emma and Hannah had been made acting assistant heads and appeared to have made a pact ahead of our meeting to turn things upside down and interrogate me.

'I'd like the assistant head position to be made permanent

and to be promoted to deputy at the beginning of the academic year,' was the opening gambit from Emma.

Hannah had broadly the same agenda.

I was a little frustrated. These interviews were supposed to be about me asking them whether they were in or out and they had completely hijacked them for their own aims. I replied in pretty much the same way to the pair of them.

I said: 'I think you have forgotten what we were supposed to be talking about today. I want to know whether you are going to, in effect, follow my vision and be part of the solution, not the problem. Instead, what you have brought me is an impossible question. I don't know you, so how can I make you a permanent assistant head and promote you to deputy in September? Not only that, I don't have the authority to do it right now. I am not actually employed in the school yet.

'I am sorry but the answer is no.'

The outcome was mixed. Hannah was furious and, as I mentally predicted, remained a thorn in my side for the whole time I was at Islington Green. Emma decided to accept what I said and stick with it. Indeed, she turned out to be a real asset. I'd give her something to get done and she'd go off and make it happen, however challenging. Once I had won her loyalty, she stuck with me all the way through and is now a principal in her own right for Lilac Sky Schools.

Teams hang together or fall apart because of loyalty and, without it, it is impossible to achieve anything.

While it is a leadership role to earn that trust and loyalty, I wanted to feel confident the people around me were dedicated to the cause and receptive to what I would be telling them. This wasn't a job where I could work with a bunch of people who were only ever prepared to go through the motions. I needed them to go the extra mile.

After meeting one-to-one with the SLT, I still had mixed feelings about what it might be possible to achieve at Islington Green. However, I had no choice now. I was committed.

I joined the school in the late spring of the 2002 academic year. The first thing I noticed when I got to my new office was that the Pink Floyd discs had disappeared. After a lengthy search and many heated denials, they were eventually found squirrelled away for 'safe keeping' at the back of the bursar's cupboard. I immediately retrieved them and put them behind my desk in just the position I had originally picked out. It made me smile every time I looked at them, which was a good thing because in those early days I had precious little else to be happy about.

Weather-wise we were in the midst of a fine May and the hot, dry days indicated we might well be blessed with a warm summer. It was obvious most of my new young charges would rather be sunning themselves outside. Indeed, after surveying the absentee rates in the register, I suspected many were. More worryingly, though, my staff seemed to be equally distracted by the upturn in the weather. As I surveyed the chaotic staff room, I saw to my dismay that the majority seemed to be dressed as though they were about to disappear off to the beach. Brightly coloured t-shirts, shorts and flip-flops had replaced the jeans they had all been sporting during my interview visit in November. Some of the staff even had sunglasses casually popped up over the crowns of their heads. They certainly didn't have the air of a professional, go-getting bunch who were ready to do business. I was also quite surprised to see many of them smoking quite openly in the staff room and corridors. Although it was a full five years before the ban on smoking in the workplace came into effect, it seemed to me this was the one place staff shouldn't need to be told to set a good example. Apparently, I was wrong and I had to issue an edict to ban all smoking in Islington Green.

I knew I had to tread carefully on the issue of work wear though. It was early days in my headship and what we wear and how we wear it is a sensitive subject. However, the visual aesthetic we present through our appearance and dress says a lot about our attitude too. While I wanted my team to be comfortable, I also wanted them to make the right impression. If everyone dressed too casually, it was quite likely the children would take this as a casual attitude to everything else in school. That was exactly the impression I didn't want the staff to make. Dressing smartly is a fast way to get instant respect.

At one of the first staff meetings, I carefully suggested the staff might all like to think about what they wore to work.

'I'm not expecting you to dress in a way that makes

you feel uncomfortable, but I would like you to look like professionals,' I said. 'Respect and confidence both start with the way you look and right now we look too casual.'

Pandemonium broke out.

There were many on the team who were appalled I had the temerity to raise this issue and one person in particular was incensed. The school's NUT rep, Ken Muller stood up then and there and made a rousing speech about a person's right to choose their own wardrobe. He questioned my right to 'force' individuals to spend their salary on a wardrobe of clothes they didn't want and, indeed, what this apparently superficial request said about my qualities as a leader. As he spoke passionately to the assembled throng, I couldn't help wondering whether he believed he was actually addressing some sort of Red Square rally instead of a bunch of cross-looking teachers. However, if I was a little taken aback by his reaction, I wasn't altogether surprised. The team was shaping up to be every bit as irascible as I had expected.

Ken's reputation preceded him. He was in his late forties and, like John Challenor, he had been at Islington Green for many years and was fiercely loyal to the school. Ken was a dyed-in-the-wool socialist who was convinced that Islington Green could be a success if it wasn't for all these modern accountabilities such as Ofsted dragging it into the mire. If there was ever a hint of dissent he would be at the head of it and he was proud of his opposition to Tony Blair, Ofsted and anything else that did not fit in with his left-wing values. Privately, I thought of him as not unlike a younger version of the socialist stalwart Tony Benn. He certainly had the Benn-like trait of staunchly sticking to his principles, even on occasions when it wasn't necessarily in his own best interests.

As I watched him addressing the staff I couldn't help thinking he wasn't the best orator in the world but, my goodness, he was incessant. Sure enough, the culmination of Ken's impassioned speech was a sit-down protest about the prospective introduction of any dress code.

I didn't force the issue. I had plenty of other things to do. I resolved to introduce the code over time, and, as the team began to see what I was trying to achieve, they did gradually fall into line and naturally smartened up. Indeed, after the half-term break, the overwhelming majority of the teaching staff came back having clearly bought smart, professional outfits, and some even proudly displayed them in my office. Ken didn't, though. Eventually, after much banter back and forth between us, we came to an unofficial agreement. He would adhere to a smart dress code for three days a week, but for at least two days a week he didn't. To make his point he wore denim trousers with his shirt and tie. I suppose he felt this gave him the respect of those around him and afforded him the independence and dignity he felt he deserved.

I could have made a big deal out of it and insisted, but I didn't. It was a straight trade-off and meant he went along with other things he might otherwise have objected to. As any sensible head knows, if you can find a way to manage the most difficult people, you'll be able to manage just about anyone. Indeed, the more difficult ones are a bit of a litmus test. If a head is doing their job well, the agitators have no grounds to work on. I was already very aware there would be a lot of times in my headship when I would need to fight, but if you fight all the time you wear yourself out. This is why you should choose your battles carefully and save your energy for the stuff that really matters. Where possible, in a difficult situation like this, a compromise is better than nothing and may even pave the way for better cooperation in the future.

What was needed was to find a way to connect with the team and show them that I was interested in what they had to say and was prepared to listen to their views. When I took over at Mayfield I instigated a system of regular informal events for small groups of staff, inviting them to meet me for tea and cakes and asking them to tell me what was wrong with the world. I always tried to inject a bit of levity and then I say, 'I will listen to your thoughts and then you can listen to the thoughts of chairman Trev.' Most people welcome the opportunity to meet the top man, although there will always be a few who are suspicious.

A series of tea-and-cake events were organised straight away at Islington Green and to begin with I told the staff a little bit about myself, which always helps to break the ice. I explained I was a single parent with two children to bring up so I understood very well the pressures that faced families.

'I'm a musician and a failed rock star, too, so I know how all you failed musicians and actors feel,' I joked.

Once the introductions were made and everyone in each group was feeling more relaxed, I asked them what they thought were the three stupidest things that happened in the school and what were the three best things. In all my years in the job, you'd have thought I'd have heard of most daft initiatives, but there is almost always something that pops up to amaze me.

After I listened to each group, I praised the best suggestions and then promised to do my best to stop at least one of the things they found daft right then and there.

Something that came up more than once during the tea-and-cake conversations at Islington Green was the Tannoy system, which was used regularly and indiscriminately and in most cases completely inappropriately. Teachers complained that it regularly interrupted lessons and that it would take ages to settle the class down after a message was broadcast.

'We'll be in the middle of a crucial inspection and some wise guy will start broadcasting an urgent plea for help because a mass brawl has started outside the science classroom,' explained Emma. 'All the pupils rush to the windows and all our good work is stuffed. It has to go.'

To make matters even worse, the system was used in conjunction with the school's CCTV network. For some strange reason, someone had once decided that at the end of the day the children should all go back to their tutor rooms to register. Most of them clearly thought this was as daft as I did but the deputies would be glued to the CCTV screens, shouting over the Tannoy at individual children they spotted in the corridors. It was all about trying to get control of something they couldn't control, but it was completely ineffectual and inappropriate.

To me, that hated public address system was no substitute for efficient management of events. I agreed with the team that it had to go and said it was going into a drawer and no one was allowed to touch it but me. The team was delighted about that.

Another thing they urged me to address was the issue of uniform. Children from Year 9 upwards were not required to wear uniform and those in the years below were given the somewhat vague requirement of 'white tops and black trousers'. I'm sure the original intention was to get them all in white polo shirts and black school trousers, but over time this had been variously interpreted as a white t-shirt/vest/hoodie and black chinos or jeans. The dress code had become so loosely observed as to be virtually non-existent. I agreed to address this mismatch as a matter of urgency.

Being a good leader means getting the balance right between the macro and micro. Leaders have to operate on two levels. They've got to take the macro view, which is the big-picture stuff, looking to strategic changes, but must also keep one eye on the micro. Those who fail are invariably the ones who think big (or kid themselves they are thinking big) yet get tripped up by overlooking the detail, or vice versa. Just listening to the team at Islington

Green made a noticeable difference. It was obvious no one had ever done so before, or at least not for a very long time. Policies and practices had just evolved over the years, but, because no one had ever talked about them, they'd been allowed to carry on even if the reasons for doing them were lost in the mists of time.

Another strategy in those first days was to instigate a programme where I watched every single teacher teach. This was something I had learned from my time as assistant head at Colne School in Brightlingsea, which I joined in 1990, when I was thirty years old. I learned a lot from the then head, Peter Upton, who had an easy and likeable manner. He had a policy of going out to watch each new teacher teach within two or three weeks of them starting at the school. This was a time before Ofsted and I remember thinking, wow, I haven't seen that done before. More importantly, I could see how buoyed up the teachers were by having the head take an interest in their classes. I heard from my colleagues that the previous head at Colne had barely left his office and that Peter's visits were like a breath of fresh air.

I introduced a similar system when I became head at Mayfield School and used to jokingly refer to it as my 'Queen's tour', but it had the same effect there. Teachers really responded well. When a head actively spends time with individual teachers it emerges pretty quickly who the good and outstanding ones are. I could leave them to carry on being good and outstanding. Others who were good but not quite brilliant could be put onto a coaching programme. At the other end of the scale are the sick, ill psychopaths who need to be moved out of the profession altogether because no one wants them near our kids.

In between these two extremes are always the teachers who are talented and great with kids but just not suited to their job. There is often a reluctance in schools to move people on, perhaps born out of political correctness or possibly because leaders just don't have the stomach for it. It shouldn't be a taboo, though. In my experience very often the people who fall into this group are frequently just waiting for someone to notice their plight. For example, this is a very common scenario among PE teachers who get too old to be interested in PE. They get up every day dreading going out on the cold, damp field. They probably didn't think that way when they were in their twenties, but, as the years roll by, they grow acutely aware of the physical demands of the job and can be pretty horrible to kids. People like this thank you for moving them on or giving them a new job.

Heads never see this unless they spend time in every classroom each year. It is easy to think you know what's going on because you see everyone in the staff room on a regular basis, but you don't. If there is one thing the Queen's tour has shown me it is that, unless you physically see teachers in the classroom, you cannot truly know about the way they teach. Most teachers are completely different when they get in front of kids in a classroom setting. Teachers who come across as bolshy and assertive in the staff room can be quite submissive with children. Ones who are interesting and funny when they chat to me may be quite dull in front of their charges. People who come across as boring or weak on the outside sometimes come alive in the classroom and have children eating out of their hands. With that final group I suspect this happens because one of the reasons people become teachers is because they are more confident at dealing with children than adults, but as a head I couldn't know this for sure unless I watched the teacher in action.

I discovered how easy it is to assume the worst while at Mayfield School. Phil, the NASUWT (National Association of Schoolmasters/Union of Women Teachers) rep, was a really awkward customer and was reluctant to follow any of the policies I tried to introduce. When I went to watch him teach his maths class, though, he was a different person completely. In fact, he was an outstanding teacher. He had some fantastic and quirky ways of holding the children's attention. He'd put two marks on the face of the class clock using a black marker pen and roar, 'Right, kids, you have three and a half minutes to complete this exercise. No one is allowed to go beyond the second mark.' It was a pleasure to watch every child in the room urgently scribbling away, occasionally casting nervous glances at the hallowed second mark. It made me view Phil in a completely different light.

Back at Islington Green, in between watching everyone teach and meeting the staff, I had to begin to take concrete steps to implement the plan I had scribbled down after my first interview. I decided very early on that

I would aim to get the majority of it done in the first 100 days. Time was of the essence and a 100-day plan would concentrate both my mind and the minds of my senior team.

My task wasn't made any easier by the fact that new issues, both large and small, popped up all the time. I'd regularly have to take time away from the main plan to sort them out, or allocate someone else to deal with the problem. Take Linda as a case in point. Linda was a dinner lady who had been at Islington Green for years. Her face was deeply lined in wrinkles and she had a permanent world-weary expression, but she never, ever stopped talking, often with a colourful turn of phrase. Staff had really taken her to heart, though, probably because she would run any errand they wanted for a few bob.

Linda clearly didn't get the memo about Islington Green being a no-smoking school now. Actually, to be more accurate, she did but chose to ignore it. Strangely, she began to light up in the cleaner's cupboard opposite the head's office.

'Linda, are you in there again?' I would shout. 'I can smell the smoke. You have to stop.'

Then, one day she came into work and all her front teeth were missing. It wasn't clear whether she had fallen over, had been in a bust-up with her husband or had simply not taken good enough care of her teeth. What was abundantly clear, though, was that she couldn't very well serve lunches to the kids looking like that. We ended up arranging – and paying for – emergency NHS treatment for Linda. It was just another thing to make happen in an already hectic schedule.

On the plus side, there were signs that the SLT was beginning to fall into line and support me after our shaky start. The regular meetings with them were starting to feel quite productive, even a little energising. There were still pockets of doubt about the job in hand, though. Indeed, as we sat in my office discussing the plan, Emma Catt voiced something that was clearly on everyone's minds.

'This 100-day plan and the list, it just seems like too big a job,' she said. 'I can't see how we can make all that happen.'

My reply was simple. I said: 'Each day you need to do one thing. That is all I am asking you to do. It is an old adage that every 1,000-mile journey starts with the first step, but it is true. You will certainly achieve a lot more than if you sit around wondering where to begin.

'Do what you can, but aim to do something transformational every day. That is the point of the 100-day plan.'

I knew I was right, too. There is little point going into a failing school and thinking, 'On the first day I will just get to know the place, see a few people and introduce myself.' No, on day one, let's specifically tell people about the strategy and then on day two start with tea and cakes with staff. Day three is the day to start going into the classes to watch the teachers. And so on.

Once people start to think this way, it is surprising what they can fit in. After all, it is a busy person you are asking to get things done, not someone who has plenty of time. Writing down action points spread over a series of days means you do get on with the task.

Of course, all of this relied on the whole team pulling with me. While I was beginning to get the trust and support of the SLT, I was still a very long way from that ideal with most of the other teachers. This was demonstrated to me in a very public way just a few days into my headship.

The first I knew of any problem was when John Challenor came into my office and said I had better go to the staff room straight away.

'What's up?' I said.

'They won't leave the staff room,' he said, adding an apologetic shrug as if to emphasise he couldn't understand it either.

'It's the end of break time,' I said, glancing somewhat superfluously at my office clock. I was actually perfectly aware of what time it was. 'Why not?'

'The staff toilet is blocked.'

'What?'

'Yes and they say they can't possibly work if there are no staff toilets.'

I got up, grabbing a few bits of paper from my desk as I walked out. As I followed John back to the staff room, I tried to get more detail about what had been going on. It transpired that the staff had all elected to stay put under union guidance.

The decision was clearly absolute nonsense, but at the

same time it went to the heart of everything that was going on at the school right then. In any challenging circumstance, the more awful the front-facing part is, the better the back bit needs to be. The toilet issue was just symbolic. The staff felt no one cared and clearly thought I was just another in a long line of heads who would come in, make little difference (or possibly even make things worse) and then move on. They believed that they warranted such little respect or concern that no one had even bothered to ensure they had the most humble of essentials, a properly decked out and working toilet.

I needed to be firm but fair. While I couldn't let them question my authority, I also had to show them I would attend to the detail.

'Good morning, everybody. I hear there is a problem with the toilets,' I said as I walked into the staff room. A sea of utterly fed up faces swivelled around to look at me.

Speaking calmly and rapidly, I went on. 'The toilets can and will be fixed, very shortly. In the meantime, I understand we have twenty-one toilets in the school, so we are going to block off some of the children's toilets, to be used by adults only.

'In addition, there is a very special, gold-plated throne room in the school. It is in my office. I will move out for the day and any of you are welcome to go there to have your cups of tea and coffee in my office and use the toilet. I don't want anyone to feel the head has a toilet and you haven't.

'Finally, I have brought with me a copy of your

terms and conditions,' I said, brandishing the entirely unconnected sheet of paper I had grabbed from my desk on the way out. 'Please go back to work, otherwise you will be in breach of contract and won't be paid for the rest of the day. Have a good day.'

On that note I left the room. I could already hear the hubbub of the teachers returning to work when Ken Muller came dashing over to catch up.

'You are kidding about the breach of contract, aren't you?' he said, slightly breathless from the exertion of chasing after me.

'Come on, Ken,' I replied, refusing to give ground. 'They're not going back to work because of the toilets? We have dozens of toilets, all over the place. Don't be silly. I will even get temporary toilets in the playground if we need to. Let's get back to work!'

The teachers did go back to work and they did come and use my toilet, which they loved. I like to think I had a humorous and positive approach to the problem. I was both firm and fair to get the job done but most importantly I did what I needed to do to make the staff feel valued. Often valuing people comes down to the simplest things, like giving them a comfortable, hassle-free work environment. However, I also wanted to prove something else, too, and that was that there is a huge difference between the leader and everyone else in the organisation. I am, as I repeatedly told my SLT team, a benevolent dictator. I had a job to do and I wasn't going to let anyone stand in my way.

What do you want to go there for?

By the end of the first week, I was exhausted. I had watched dozens of teachers teach, had tea and cakes till I was fit to burst, solved the toilet crisis and talked until my throat hurt. On the Friday morning I had to go to a meeting on the way to the school. It wasn't far away but, worried about running late, I hailed a black cab to take me back to Islington Green.

'Islington Green School,' I said confidently to the driver as I climbed into the back seat.

'Islington Green School?' the driver laughed throatily. 'Are you sure? What do you want to go there for?'

'I am the new head,' I said, doing my best not to sound too pompous.

'Yeah, well, you want a bloody medal taking that on, you do,' he went on, barely pausing for breath. 'You heard that Pink Floyd song, "We Don't Need No Education"? They done that in there and they bloody mean it too. Bunch of bloody tearaways. They bloody need educating, I can tell you.'

I let his prattle wash over me. I didn't need to reply anyhow. He had started what was clearly one of his regular routines and I saw no reason to stop him. Mercifully the ride was quite short and we quickly arrived at the by now familiar school gate.

'How much is that?' I asked, reaching in my pocket for my wallet as soon as I had stepped out of the cab.

'Nah, you keep your money,' he said, with grin and a dismissive wave of his hand. Then, with a nod in the direction of the school, he added, 'Son, you need every penny you can get trying to sort out that place.'

With that he gave another throaty laugh and roared off, no doubt to begin whatever well-worn comedy routine his next victim instigated.

Chapter three

FLOOD THE SCHOOL WITH POSITIVITY

When I was a deputy head at Alec Hunter in the early nineties and keen to make my mark, I read a piece in the *TES* (*Times Educational Supplement*) about assertive discipline that really got me thinking. The idea, which was in its infancy back then, was based on some research done in America by Lee and Marlene Canter that advocated a structured, systematic approach to managing poor behaviour in classrooms. After spending time monitoring 10,000 lessons, the pair said that a firm but positive manner with clearly established rules would see children better engaged in the learning process. In other words, if pupils and teachers weren't distracted by misbehaviour in the classroom, they could all get on with the job in hand. Positive recognition changes people's behaviour while sanctions just contain it for a short while.

At that time, only two schools in the whole of the UK had embraced the theory. One was in Liverpool and the other, coincidently, was a school in Islington. It was Highbury Grove, though, rather than Islington Green. Away from these two schools, the consensus was that this theory was not the way forward. Critics said it was too Pavlovian to tell children that if they behaved well they would get a reward while if they misbehaved they'd be punished. There was a cartoon in the *TES* depicting children as cattle being prodded because they had done something wrong. Everyone seemed firmly wedded to the mindset of the seventies and eighties: children would find their own way of learning and behaving.

I wasn't so sure and certainly didn't think the theory should be dismissed out of hand. I started looking into the Canters' research in more detail and, the more I read, the more I liked. It seemed to me they had some very valid points.

The way they had classified how teachers acted in the classroom, for example, resonated strongly with my own experience at Alec Hunter. The Canters distinguished three styles of teaching: non-assertive, hostile and assertive. Non-assertive teachers are those who use a timid, pleading style in a non-directive manner. Say, for example, a teacher wanted certain members of his class to settle down at the beginning of a lesson. In the non-assertive style he might say, 'Could we possibly sit down and make a start? Please, John?'

Hardly surprisingly, usually children don't take much

notice of these entreaties. Any teacher who is submissive in this way automatically hands over control to the other people in the room.

At the other end of the scale is the hostile style. Here a teacher begins from the stance that students are adversaries and the only way to get through to them is via an abrasive, combative style: 'You, boy, what do you think you are doing? Sit down and shut up.'

The boy in question, having been asked what he thinks he is doing, inevitably answers back with a confrontational 'Nothing, sir, I wasn't doing anything.' The reply only leads to further exchange, distraction and time wasting.

The final option, and the one advocated by the Canters, is the assertive mode. In the same scenario, a teacher may say, 'Sit down, John, there's a good boy. Face this way.'

If it is said in a voice that sounds like the speaker means it, it is very effective.

Speech, or how you say things, is at the core of positive discipline. The Canters were absolutely right in their observation that the way some teachers speak to their pupils often makes a bad situation worse. For example, one of the nuances of the English language is that we frequently couch our expressions as questions when we don't really need an answer at all. It is quite common, for example, for a teacher to say, 'How many times have I told you to stop that?'

In their head the teacher is clearly meaning the expression as an instruction; however, in a child's mind it could easily be heard as a question, inviting the potential response 'lots'.

These nuances in language need to be addressed as part of a move to teaching in a more assertive, direct and positive way. Changing the way we speak doesn't come easily to anyone. It takes practice and coaching, just the same way as footballers need practice and coaching to work on the skills specific to their employment. It helps teachers to have pre-prepared scripts to use in the classroom that map out responses according to particular scenarios. These scripts are not particularly complicated and simply present alternative ways of talking to a class.

Positive interaction relies on saying what you want rather than what you don't want, and it can have a powerfully positive effect on behaviour. Using commands such as 'don't' or 'stop' clouds children's understanding of the positive outcome you want them to achieve. Positive language yields positive results.

Buoyed up by my research, I got in touch with John Bayley, the one and only trainer in the UK who specialised in the Canters' work at that time, and invited him to meet with me. He explained more about what he'd been doing and he also put me in touch with the heads at the two schools in London and Liverpool that were embracing the theory. I subsequently visited both schools and a seminar John ran in London to showcase assertive discipline. Within a matter of weeks, John visited Alec Hunter and trained a group of staff there. He showed us how we should balance incentives for positive behaviour with disciplinary rules, and he explained how to speak to children to encourage the responses we wanted. As I became more familiar with the style, I made some small adaptations to close what I believed to be gaps in the theory and called my version 'positive discipline'.

The biggest problem I had with the original theory was that there wasn't a firm enough exit strategy in the behaviour plan. The series of penalties for bad behaviour was very clear: for example, a child might get their name on the board for misbehaving, be given a two-minute stay behind after lessons for a further infraction and perhaps a detention after school at the next level. The Canters' final, emergency, clause was that a child would be 'exited from the room'. To me this seemed a little vague. Where is the exit, I wondered? Where do these children go? It gave the impression there was a group of administrators waiting to scoop up these exited children, but what would happen in a school of fifty classes if one child from each class got exited? How would the school deal with that volume of children?

Likewise, I also realised that more thought needed to be given to the possibility that teachers might deliberately race through the warning system so they could exit the awkward or disruptive kids at the earliest opportunity. It was something I fully expected to happen, and I believed some provision needed to be put in place to make sure teachers were applying the system fairly and appropriately. Plus, I didn't believe it would be enough to simply introduce the concept of rewarding good behaviour. I might say to the team, 'Here is the system of rewards – please use them generously,' but there were no guarantees the team would do so. Just because there was a new system didn't mean it would definitely be used. In my view there had to be an additional mechanism to nudge the team towards giving copious rewards.

That said, the Canters' core principles were spot on and I resolved to introduce them as quickly as possible and refine them as I went along to address any gaps that revealed themselves.

The concept of positive discipline heralded a light-bulb moment for me. As soon as I introduced it, Alec Hunter school calmed down overnight. Teachers, parents and even pupils were very excited about it and I was the most excited out of the lot of them. It felt like I had unlocked some long-held secret. There were so many positive knock-on effects from this improved behaviour, too, over and above the fact that children were now in the right frame of mind and able to absorb their lessons. The school was a far better environment for teachers to work in and incidents of bullying among pupils were reduced considerably. Why doesn't everyone do this, I thought?

Then, suddenly and unexpectedly, results dropped off a cliff. After a few months of incredible across-the-board improvements, everything ground to a halt. Indeed, almost overnight, behaviour actually got worse than it had been before we began. Everyone in the staff room was tearing their hair out in frustration.

'What's happened?' they demanded. 'Why has it all stopped working?'

I felt a bit stumped. How had something that had initially performed brilliantly descended so rapidly into a disaster?

Flood the school with positivity

I suspected, although I wasn't yet sure, the problem lay with the reward system. At the core of positive discipline is a need for an approach that balances positive and negative. Thus, if a student does well, they will receive some sort of reward such as a merit mark or a point in some other system that leads up to a meaningful prize.

The other side of this scenario is the need for an effective system to deal with negative, or bad, behaviour in a way that introduces the least disruption possible to the flow of a lesson. One of the most common ways to do this is to put names on the board, which reduces the need to stop the lesson to issue a full reprimand. The idea is that writing a name on the board should be done in a calm, non-degrading manner with the main aim being to provide an efficient record-keeping system rather than humiliate the pupil.

My hunch was it had all gone wrong because it is human nature to focus on the negative. Without the balance of the positive, this whole system breaks down. Positive recognition via merits and rewards makes children feel good about themselves and makes them less likely to misbehave in the first place. To test my assumption, I decided to sit in on a few lessons.

The first class I went to was a real eye opener. It was a geography lesson and it was clear from the moment I opened the door that the class was in chaos. The teacher was a young man who had only been with the school for a couple of years. When I walked in, he was writing a child's name on the board under a long list of names.

At the top of the list was a large cross indicating that the names below were being reprimanded for bad behaviour. On the other side of the board there was a large tick to note the children who had behaved well or made some sort of positive contribution to the class. There were no names below the large tick and it looked rather isolated and forlorn.

It was difficult to concentrate because the room had erupted at the addition of the name, but a quick tot-up of the list revealed that it included twenty-seven names. That meant that twenty-seven pupils out of a class of thirty had their names on the board for misbehaving. I only needed one look at the baying mob of kids and it was easy to see what they were trying to do. They were aiming for the jackpot: 100 per cent of names on the board for misbehaviour.

'Here, Sir, look what Billy is doing.'

'Billy, stop that,' said the exasperated teacher.

Billy's name soon became number twenty-eight on the board and the class erupted once again.

By focussing on the negative and forgetting to reward children for their good behaviour, this teacher had completely reversed the idea of positive discipline. Unwittingly, he had created a scenario where children felt *encouraged* to behave badly.

Although an extreme instance, this was not an isolated example. I quickly discovered that the reason things had broken down at Alec Hunter was because the carefully-laid-out guidelines had slowly descended into focussing on the negative. Children weren't getting any benefits from behaving well, so they sought recognition in the only way presented to them.

One thing children are always best at knowing is whether something is fair or not. It is as though they have done a PhD in Fairology at an unfeasibly early age. The positive discipline system is very fair and, if teachers stick to it and are meticulous in praising good behaviour rather than focussing on the bad, they will win their pupils' respect and understanding.

Children need to know beforehand what is expected of them in the classroom, which is why we need rules and clearly set out consequences of both positive and negative behaviour. That way children know what will happen if they follow the rules and are equally aware of the consequences if they don't. By offering them these choices, children will be left in no doubt that their actions have an impact and this helps them learn self-discipline and responsible behaviour. Best of all, the system is completely fair. For all this to work smoothly, though, children have to clearly see the results of their actions. For positive discipline to be effective, every child who has behaved well should have a positive reward at the end of the lesson.

Interestingly, children are usually far more welcoming towards the concept of positive discipline than teachers. Changing the way a teacher speaks and interacts with their class is not easy and requires continuous effort, which some staff are simply not prepared to commit to without constant pressure. Over time I developed a number of strategies to keep positive discipline on track and make sure it is happening correctly. The simplest way is to do learning walks, or spot checks, which means travelling around the school to see what everyone is doing.

If I can see that resolve is flagging, or teachers are swinging towards the discipline side of the equation, I find that recruiting the kids at the earliest stage can be really helpful to keep things on track.

Tell children at assembly they will get a reward at the end of the week when a teacher fills a form in and you can rest assured they won't let the matter drop. Otherwise, left to their own devices, a fair proportion of teachers may 'forget' to submit their records.

Something that worked really well at Alec Hunter was introducing a specific well-publicised merit week. The school was plastered in posters and I talked about it at assembly and every chance I got.

'Kids, if you haven't been given your merits, now is the time to catch up.'

To add grist to the mill, I produced a league table of departments showing which had given out the most merits – and woe betide the ones that had given out virtually none. This approach may be judged as car-crash management, but it does work. After a few years of relentless campaigning, the system did become part of the routine, but even then I never left it unchecked.

I learned a lot of lessons introducing positive discipline at Alec Hunter and refined the programme further during my headship at Mayfield. It seemed to me that Islington Green would also benefit considerably from it too. The school had certainly fallen into a dangerous cycle where the focus on the discipline side of things had been ratcheted up to a point where it was entirely inappropriate. Worse still, it was having no effect whatsoever.

The proof of the over-reliance on stick rather than carrot was in the eye-watering number of exclusions. In the previous five terms before I arrived, no fewer than 750 children had been locked out, 410 of them in the past year alone.

Marion Parsons' often quoted view was that there was a limit to how much time could be spent addressing bad behaviour in some children, particularly when it was clearly at the expense of others. She believed it was easier to get both children and parents to take things seriously with a fixed-term exclusion.

This was far too gung ho for me. Exclusions were being used far too readily and far too early in the sanction process. Kids were getting taken out of school for answering back when they had mobile phones confiscated or their baseball caps taken away. At this school there was no such thing as 'three strikes and you're out'. Here, after one, two tops, it was game over. There was seemingly no thought given to how to adjust the behaviour or to the impact the exclusions were having on children and their families.

For a positive discipline strategy to be effective, schools need to be very clear on the consequences of misbehaviour. It is wholly inappropriate to go straight to exclusion, or indeed to use exclusion as a threat at all. Ideally there should be no more than five tiers of consequences for misbehaviour. For example, the first time a child misbehaves they will be warned, the second they may be asked to stay for five minutes at the end of the lesson, the third may mean a lunchtime detention, the fourth a meeting with the head of year and the fifth a meeting with the head. It is vital that the consequences are not psychologically, or physically, harmful to pupils or used in an inappropriate way.

At the beginning of my second week at Islington Green, I gathered the staff together in the library to outline my vision of positive discipline. It wouldn't have been my preferred destination for any sort of meeting as it was such a smelly, ill-thought-out, scruffy room, but everyone seemed pretty comfortable in there. This was despite the fact that June, the librarian, was someone who never made any effort to make anyone feel welcome in 'her' space, and that went doubly so for me for some reason. When I told her about the meeting she looked doubtful but in a show of forced magnanimity said I could use the projector screen that hung at one end of the room.

'You'll have to bring your own projector, though,' she added.

'Don't worry, I have my own,' I said, trying my hardest to remain friendly.

I had bought my own projector some years earlier, at great expense. It was about two feet wide and weighed a ton and would be laughable by today's standards, but back then I was quite proud of it and would resolutely lug it everywhere it was needed.

I set up the projector and waited while the team ambled in, musing to myself that I really would need to do something about this room. Some of the teachers were perched two to a chair on shabby and worn furniture, while others took up strategic positions skulking behind bookshelves.

To set the mood I asked the group a question.

'What is it you'd like a child to do?' I asked, looking around the room. I could already see a number of the teachers frowning. 'I don't mean in terms of their learning. No, what I am referring to is the way you'd like them to behave.'

For a few moments there was silence, then a few teachers offered their thoughts.

'Show me respect.'

'Make the best of their own learning.'

'Enjoy the environment.'

These were the sort of meaningless replies I was expecting. Although it is a simple question, truth be told, no one ever really thinks about what it is they'd like from their classes. They've never defined in their own minds what it is they actually want their charges to do.

'How about: sit down and do what they've been asked to do?' I said. 'Or, more succinctly: do as they are told.'

Amazingly, I could see several teachers around the room nodding enthusiastically. A few were even making comments to their colleagues clearly approving of the suggestion.

I did my best not to betray any of the frustration I felt that this idea should be such a revelation to degree-educated individuals. My new colleagues at Islington Green were not alone, though. In more than two decades in this profession I've come across the problem time and again. Teachers always assume children will instinctively know how to behave because they should somehow automatically understand the rules about what they should be doing. Yet, the reason this theory breaks down is that, for the most part, there are *no rules* to follow. This was certainly the case at Islington Green, as I discovered.

When I had arrived at Islington Green I had asked John Challenor for a copy of the school rules.

'I'm not sure there are any,' he replied.

'What, none at all?' I asked, disbelievingly. Most schools have at least some rules, even if they are simply left mouldering in a drawer.

'There may have been some once,' he said doubtfully. 'I don't remember any, though.'

'How do the children know how to behave, then?'

'Well, I think they broadly know how to behave,' he began, but then checked himself. We both knew many of the children at Islington Green patently didn't know how to behave. Some did, but most didn't.

The rules I was most keen to find were *behavioural* ones, which govern codes of conduct in the classroom. These are not the same as *school* rules, which invariably don't come close to addressing classroom behaviour. Indeed, in my experience, school rules fall into three categories: classroom rules, community laws and aspirational ideas. Classroom rules cover what you are allowed to do in class, while the community ones cover stuff like no chewing gum, walk on the left, don't wear hats and so on. They are sometimes helpful and sometimes unhelpful because they have often fallen into abeyance and people don't really follow them anyway. When they do, they tend to follow them over-zealously and dramatic confrontations often result.

The aspirational rules (which incidentally are usually found in the schools with the worst behavioural problems) are the ones often described as 'philosophy' or 'core values'. They are usually a complete hodgepodge and talk rather vaguely about expecting children to 'be great citizens' or 'find their learning style'. They are all teacher-speak for not very much.

The rules that were really needed at Islington Green were behavioural ones for the classroom. In fact only a few basic ones were needed. The first was for children to follow teachers' instructions. Something like 'Do what you are told, when you are told' would be sufficient. It is the top thing that we want children to do in the classroom. If that rule isn't in place, they won't follow all the rest.

My next rule was: 'Listen in silence'. Frequently, general school rules may say something about respecting the teacher and not shouting, but actually what we all want is for children to listen to the teacher and listen to each other, too. A key behavioural tool is getting children to be silent for at least some part of the class. Teachers don't always do it. In my first week of sitting in on lessons at Islington Green I would often walk into a classroom and find the teacher was inexplicably not insisting on silence.

More than once I said to the teachers, 'You have to wait on silence. It will come. Indeed, demand silence by modelling it and standing at the front in silence yourself.'

Another rule I advocated was an adaptation from the Canters' work: 'Keep hands, feet and rude comments to yourself.' In other words, don't punch people, don't kick people and don't tell them to 'eff off'.

I explained to the group of teachers gathered in the library that each one in this handful of classroom rules we would now be following at Islington Green was positively redirectional. They focussed on the behaviour a teacher wants, not the behaviour they don't want. Thus, instead of saying, 'Katie, how many times have I told you to stop talking?' a more effective way to stop the pupil talking would be: 'Katie, we are all listening now. Remember rule number two? There's a good girl.'

It might sound patronising, I admitted to the team, but it works.

After letting the behavioural rules sink in, I now had to outline how we were going to encourage the children to follow them.

'This school has lost its way and it needs direction,' I began. 'More specifically, the children need direction and that won't be achieved by resorting to punishments all the time. The reason we are here today is to outline the measures we are going to introduce to improve discipline without having to resort to excluding pupils.

'We are starting a merits system, which will reward both attendance and good behaviour. Students will be issued with books and you will award them merits for good work and behaviour. They will be encouraged to build up a number of merits that can be exchanged for rewards.

'I am also proposing introducing a Fast Pass system that ties in with the merits. This will be similar to the Fast Pass system you get at theme parks, where you pay extra to slip into the front of the queue. Here you don't have to pay anything, you just have to behave yourself and build up some merits. Sixth-form students will have to build up 100 merits to get a Fast Pass that will allow them to leave the school at lunch time. As you know, the whole school has been allowed to come and go freely at lunchtime in the past and it has been a nightmare. There have been fights, petty thefts and bad behaviour, which does very little to help our reputation in the local community. From now on, anyone wanting to go out at lunch time will need to have shown exemplary behaviour.'

There were worried glances from some teachers who were clearly wondering how we were going to police this new draconian lunchtime rule.

'Don't worry – I will be organising a rota on the school gates to enforce this and I myself will be going out there too,' I said.

Before the group had time to protest or argue, I ploughed on.

'For the younger ones in Year 7 and Year 8, merits will go towards a Fast Pass that will get them into the canteen before the bigger kids. It can be really difficult for the little ones in the lunch queue, so this will give them an incentive to behave well.'

'Lunchtimes are also far too long. I know you need a good period of time to get 1,050 kids through, but one hour twenty minutes is too much. They've all finished well before that and there is chaos. My proposal is to gradually reduce the time to forty-five minutes, or fewer. We will provide incentives to smooth that through, including TVs and computers in the lunch hall. We'll also move to a two-shift lunch.'

There was a palpable aura of shock around the room.

'The easiest way to get any child to be quiet is to turn on the TV, so let's give them TV at lunch time. They are busy all day long, so why not. As for computers, don't worry; I can pretty much guarantee they won't smash them up.'

After outlining the series of rewards, I came to the punishment side.

'Exclusions are going to stop,' I said firmly. 'It is a completely unreasonable policy and they don't work. Instead, we are going to set up an exclusion room. If children are disruptive, they can be sent to the exclusion room for a set period rather than being suspended. We will organise a rota to supervise the room.'

Flood the school with positivity

After I had finished talking, there was an uncharacteristic hush in the room as the staff absorbed the new regime. I could tell there was a healthy scepticism among at least half that these measures would work. Interestingly, though, a large number, perhaps as much as a quarter, were nodding and whispering animatedly to their colleagues. They had clearly found something inspirational in what I had to say.

Something I had on my side was that one of the things that characterises those who choose to work in a troubled inner-city school is a firm belief that something can be done. I was offering a fresh outlook and a way that things might succeed with a little effort. Many of the staff were bright enough to see it was worth their while to give it a go.

That is not to say there were not lingering doubts, even among those who could see the merits in what I was saying.

'I like the concept of positive discipline, but I think we need to be a lot more prescriptive on the detail,' said Ian, our young IT teacher. 'We need to nail down exactly how this will work.'

A number of his colleagues nodded in agreement.

'It seems there is a lot of room for interpretation,' agreed Anita, a languages teacher. 'How can we be sure to be consistent? Surely this thing sinks or swims through us being consistent.'

'I am aware it seems like there is a bit of creative ambiguity,' I agreed. 'The trouble is, we can't start out with the whole nine yards mapped out perfectly. My experience of introducing positive discipline at Mayfield, my previous school, is it developed over time and we had to adapt as circumstances dictated. I fully expect that to be our experience here. We can't wait until it is completely mapped out before we begin. We have to get started now, because we don't have the luxury of time here.

'I don't want people to get upset about this, or stressed and anxious, or to start blaming each other, blaming me and blaming other people. We are all trying this together and if it doesn't work we will change it. If it needs tweaking, we will tweak it. If it is great, we will carry on. But we have to give it a go.'

That was the way I approached all my meetings with the team, and I found most of them were quite comfortable with it. I'm not the type to insist something has to work in a certain, highly prescriptive, way. It is one way of managing a team, but it is not my way and I don't think it would have worked at Islington Green anyway.

Even though I could tell that many of the team weren't convinced, the majority agreed to give the system a chance. Two of the most highly unionised teachers did, however, make it quite clear they didn't agree with the initiative and indicated they would not be following the carefully-laid-out plan. I had to explain to them that, while I respected their position as conscientious objectors, they were contractually obliged to do anything the head asked.

The same had happened with Paul, the NUT rep at Alec Hunter, so I wasn't altogether surprised. I went to see him teach three times. The first time I could see he wasn't taking any notice of what I had said about positive discipline. I told him he really needed to follow the policy and he said, 'Right, right.' The second time he admitted quite openly that he didn't believe children should be given rewards for good behaviour and that, even if they should, he didn't have time to administer them. After the third time I sent him a disciplinary warning letter that said he had to follow my instructions and after that he did.

The crux of the problem was that most of the teachers at Islington Green had been reliant on the ultimate sanction of exclusions for so long. It was going to be a tough habit to break. Indeed, I almost suspected that many had fallen into a vicious cycle. Pupils knew that if they pressed the right buttons a teacher would kick them out for the slightest behavioural infringement and the teachers obliged because it was much easier to get rid of disruptive children at the earliest opportunity.

It wasn't long before I was proved right. Within hours of outlining the new rewards-and-punishments strategy, a teacher called Kevin stormed into my office demanding that I exclude a pupil.

'He attacked me,' Kevin said.

'Well, if that is the case, I would take it very seriously,' I began slowly, wondering which part of the 'no exclusions' instruction he had missed at the earlier meeting. 'Tell me what happened.'

'Jimmy has been acting up all lesson,' he said, speaking rapidly, his eyes wide with the injustice of it all. 'I told him several times that if he didn't behave I would be sending him to see you and he faced exclusion. He said he didn't effing care. The next time I told him, do you know what he did?'

'No, what did he do?' I asked, my heart sinking as I imagined the entire scenario.

'He got to his feet and said he was going to see you anyhow.'

'OK, so what happened then?'

'Well, he just gets up and I told him to stay where he was...'

'And?'

'I stood in front of the door and he barged right into me. Pushed me aside like I was nothing. That's assault that is.'

I sighed. Even though Kevin had done his best to present himself in the best possible light, I disagreed with his take on the version of events entirely. A teacher's job is to manage children to get them to do what the teacher wants them to do, not to threaten and provoke them until they feel they have no choice but to leave the room. If a teacher dives in front of them in this situation, that teacher will be barged out of the way. It is inevitable, but it isn't an attack.

At the meeting just a few hours earlier I had made it very clear that there was a no-touching rule in the school. Under no circumstances was a teacher to physically engage with the children in any way whatsoever. After exclusions, confiscation was apparently one of the favourite means of discipline and punishment at Islington Green and it often led to physical confrontation. In the few days I had been at the school I had regularly witnessed teachers snatching property away from the children. The top item targeted for confiscation was baseball caps, which had become very fashionable right then. Kids wanted to wear them but they weren't part of the school uniform. Foolhardy teachers would simply lift them off a child's head, which I always felt was a huge invasion of privacy. The hat may have been worthless, it may even have looked ridiculous, but that kid owned it. They chose the colour and they wanted to look cool, but a teacher just snatched it away and worse still put it somewhere where the child couldn't even look at it. This reaction always has a big psychological impact.

Teachers should never snatch hats, or indeed anything else, in the first place and physically fronting up a child to stop them leaving a room is even worse. No one should physically engage with children and I have always been very clear about that in my schools. It is wrong and the attacker is always going to come off worse. In difficult schools the kid will naturally go to push the adult away and before anyone knows it teachers will be accusing the kid of assault and vice versa.

'I'm not going to punish the child,' I told Kevin. 'I'm going to talk to the parents and when they say the teacher shouldn't have done that I'm going to have to agree with them. There is no circumstance where it is acceptable to physically intervene with a pupil.'

Kevin looked stunned and it was obvious he didn't

agree with me. In the weeks that followed he repeatedly came to see me to demand that I exclude this pupil or that. Eventually I had to threaten to discipline him. If I had given in and excluded a child it would have been a case of a weak teacher being supported by a weak head. I didn't want that.

Chapter four

NO BELL PRIZE

There was a permanent feeling of chaos during my first few weeks at Islington Green. Even my office, which should have offered some sort of refuge from the mayhem outside, was not immune. It was on a corridor that acted as a cut-through for most of the children and, as I had surmised at my interview, the five doors offered them ample opportunity to burst in. And burst in they did. A lot.

I had to resolve that situation fast, and not just for my own sanity either. It was going to be impossible to have a quiet chat with anyone, whether school inspectors, a government official or a parent, if I was under constant threat of invasion. I immediately had four of the five doors blocked off and installed my PA, Anne Davis, outside the remaining one as my gatekeeper. I had to have control of who came in to see me and when they did it.

Anne, as I discovered, was every bit as much of an

asset as Brenda Steele had been at Mayfield. She was already at the school when I arrived and had the rather bizarre title of Marion's 'confidential typist'. I never really got to the bottom of this, but suspected that it had been because the others in the admin section wouldn't countenance anyone having a better job title and that, as they were a vocal lot, Marion had relented. I warmed to Anne straight away. She was in her late fifties and was small in stature but with a big personality. She'd listen well then tell you exactly what she thought. She was also extremely loyal, which is something I prize highly.

I decided pretty much as soon as I arrived that I wanted her to be my PA, but I was a little concerned whether it might be too much for her. Anne was very willing to work but she did have an air of permanent exhaustion about her. It was only when I probed further that I found out why. She was so badly paid at Islington Green, earning less than £9,000 a year, that when she finished there at 5pm she used to work at a local publishing company until 9 or 10pm, to make up her wages.

'I want you to stop doing the job in the evenings,' I said, after I called her into my office for a chat.

She looked crestfallen.

'I have to do it,' she said. 'I love this job, but I can't afford to live on what I get here.'

'How much do you get from the publishers?'

'It works out at about £7,000 a year, on top of my basic at Islington Green.'

'If I could make sure you get another £7,000 from your salary here, would you stop working there?'

'Would I heck? Absolutely.'

Her eyes lit up as she said this. For years she'd been waiting for this break. I managed to work everything out by shifting things around a bit and also getting her a position as clerk to the governors. It meant she had to do the odd meeting after school each week, but her quality of life improved overnight. Plus, of course, I had secured her utter loyalty.

While I sorted out my PA and the door situation, I also tackled the head's office itself. I wanted to get rid of all the unwanted clutter and keep it clear of the mounds of paper that seem to plague most heads' offices. It was very important that when anyone came to see me my office projected the right impression. I always judge people by their environment. If the office is in chaos, with papers strewn around and dirty cups abandoned in corners, it says a lot about the person who works there.

At the same time as I fortified my office, I had it in mind to block off other entrances along the ground-floor corridor outside, making this an adults-only area by diverting the kids elsewhere.

It might seem like a draconian solution, but right then the children at that school didn't have the emotional intelligence to understand they couldn't just burst in to the offices unannounced. It wasn't their fault. The previous layout was appalling and they were just following the lead of countless children before them. Changing the layout didn't mean that they weren't welcome, even encouraged, to speak to us when necessary. However, the new arrangement symbolised that the office area was an official place of work and had to be treated with due respect. Rules needed to be followed.

Recalling my experience the first time I came to the school, for my interview, I knew it was imperative to change the way people came into the school too. The current arrangement created entirely the wrong impression for visitors, who had to run the gauntlet of 1,050 unruly children just to get into the reception area of the school. As I knew from experience, not many Islington Green kids were prepared to step back to let an adult in first and they didn't see much call to curb their language just because there was a visitor. Again, it wasn't totally their fault. Things had always been like this and they knew no other way. We needed separate entrances for parents and visitors and for children.

Working quickly, I had managed to wrangle a not insubstantial £3.5 million investment made up of grants from various government bodies. There was some asbestos that needed removing and the lighting was terrible, so, while it took a lot of paperwork to it, there was money available. After that I called in an architect called Andy Gollifer and charged him with doing what he could to make the dreadful school building better. I told him that we needed both short- and long-term solutions. My avowed aim was to eventually get rid of the seven-storey building and replace it with something more manageable and appropriate, but for now I had to make what we did have fit for purpose.

Andy's design for the ground-floor corridors presented the perfect opportunity to create two separate entrances. The original one was refurbished and made into the visitor entrance, while knocking a hole through a wall further down the courtyard created a new door into an area that would be known as Student Services. This initiative gave me the opportunity to completely change the arrangement around the student entrance too. Traditionally, all the administration staff had been arranged around the entrance, but there really was no need to have them there. All the kids needed was one, preferably popular, member of staff to deal with all the student issues with the back of house staying, well, back of house.

The teachers immediately dubbed the now separated area around the head's office 'the corridor of power', but the SLT and other members of staff who worked there were delighted. For the first time in years they were able to get on with their jobs without a constant threat of interruption.

'It feels a lot more special when you go to the head's office now,' Sally, one of the younger teachers, told me. 'Before there were loads of kids hanging around and it was like anywhere else in the school.'

She was right. The layout immediately commanded respect from the kids who were taken there because they had misbehaved. They knew it was serious. It also had an important role in the positive discipline rewards system because children who came to my office for a clap on the back knew it really meant something important.

I found that one of the most difficult things about being a head of a challenging school is finding a way to interact effectively with *all* the kids, not just the disruptive ones. At Islington Green there were around 100 pupils who had significant emotional and intellectual needs, but that left 950 who didn't. Not all of them were destined for top universities, but they were normal in most ways.

In those early days in particular, I found nearly every working hour taken up with kids who had assaulted a teacher, or sworn at them, or run out of school. I'd either be talking to the kids themselves or their parents, or discussing an action plan with teachers. A thought kept reoccurring: how do I get to see the good kids?

The positive discipline system seemed like an obvious place to start and I focussed on a way to meet children who were showing the best behaviour. Trial and error at my previous schools had already shown me that most kids don't like getting their merit certificates in assembly so we had devised a system where they'd collect them from the head of year. If they got a stage further they'd get their certificates from the deputy head. If they got the highest possible marks in the merit structure, they were invited to collect their certificate from the head's office. I decided to instigate this new system at Islington Green and this is where the new layout played a part. By being invited to the corridor of power, the kids immediately felt like they had done something important. They were being invited into the 'adult area' to receive praise from the head.

In the first year of this system I saw half a dozen kids, and as time went on the number rose to around 100. Pretty soon Anne had to introduce a booking system. It was fantastic for me, though. I finally got to meet all the nice, able kids in a calm, organised manner and have a few words with them without fear of interruption. It wasn't just positive for them; it was positive for me too.

Blocking off the doors in the corridor of power and changing the entrances were just the start of the physical changes I wanted to make at Islington Green. I have discovered over the years that the environment can have a huge impact on the behaviour and performance of children. If pupils feel they go to a scruffy, chaotic school, their behaviour will reflect that. The seven-storey monolith that was Islington Green presented huge challenges in every way, but that didn't mean there was nothing that could be done. Indeed, even though Andy and I were working on big plans for how we might eventually completely rebuild the school, there were a number of other quick wins to be had. I set about putting them in motion straight away. One of the first was to give the public areas a much-needed lick of paint.

Over the years I have become known as the head that paints his schools lilac. The root of this story goes back to when I became head at Mayfield School back in 1996 and inherited a horrible old school building. It was obvious no money had been spent on it for years and years. I went over to sort a few things out before my official start date and the caretaker popped in to introduce himself. He said the old headmaster hadn't redecorated the whole time he was there, so would I like my office to be given a lick of paint?

In the ensuing discussion over what colour I would like in my new office, I chose lilac. Right then I had no particular preference for the colour. However, as I sought inspiration, my eyes fell upon the seats that were already there, which were lilac. I noticed the carpet too was flecked with the same colour.

'Well, I haven't learned much from my wife when it comes to design, but one thing she has taught me is to pick out the colours in the room,' I told the caretaker. 'What about something to match the lilac here in the carpet and on the chairs?'

The caretaker nodded, but I could tell he had reservations.

'Aren't you worried it is, er, well, a little poofy?' he said at long last, clearly agonising on how best to put it.

'Don't worry – I am in touch with my feminine side,' I laughed, although I could tell he was still a bit reticent.

I did think it a little odd, though. A colour is just a colour. I could never understand why people interpret some colours as more effeminate or 'poofy' than others. It is faintly ridiculous when you think about it.

The room had been duly decorated in a lovely shade of lilac by the time I started at Mayfield a few weeks later.

Then a curious thing happened. Within a few weeks of me starting, some of the office staff asked whether they could have their areas painted too. Then the caretaker asked for permission to paint lilac over some graffiti in the main corridor. After that, the demand for lilac exploded, which was just as well because it turned out the caretaker had mistakenly got in a job lot of 100 litres of lilac paint. It didn't stop there either. Teachers began to wear lilac shirts, ties, dresses and skirts. To begin with, I wondered whether they were taking the mickey, but gradually it dawned on me that they were wearing it out of loyalty to the school.

After a while we kitted the kids out in purple blazers too and they looked fantastic. People started to tell me that the colour was having a calming effect. I wasn't sure whether it was the influence of the colour or the other work we were doing on positive discipline, but I certainly wasn't going to complain if the colour had played a part.

The next inspector who visited Mayfield could not help but note the prevalence of lilac. Her tone was one of approval.

'I've seen some research on this,' she told me earnestly. 'Apparently lilac is one of the colours you see on the horizon when the sun sets and it has a very calming effect. Is that the reasoning behind it?'

'Well, yes, that is certainly one of the reasons,' I nodded enthusiastically, not daring to mention that the origins of the lilacification lay in the colour of my office carpet. We had only found its calming properties after we had painted the whole school in lilac.

Naturally I decided to export the lilac branding to Islington Green. It seemed to me that, whether or not the calming properties were a scientific fact, we needed all the help we could get. My office was duly painted in lilac and kitted out with lilac chairs and sofas. Then the caretaking team began to work their way through the corridors and classrooms, slowly transforming everything into a pleasant shade of lilac.

While sorting out the entrances, converting the head's office and giving the rest of the school a lilac spruce-up sent a strong message that there was new management in town, I couldn't leave things there. There was a great deal of work that needed doing in other areas of the school that looked like they hadn't been touched for decades. I was also acutely aware that, if I didn't move quickly, I would open myself to criticism that all I was doing was spending thousands of pounds on feathering my own nest while everyone else worked in squalor. So, one of the first places I turned my attention to was the staff room.

It was a truly horrible place and if anything it had even deteriorated since Marion had shown it to me during my interview. I wandered in after school to try to get an idea of what to do with it.

Looking at the walls, I couldn't help but let out an audible sigh. They were lined with noticeboards, my absolute pet hate. Every school coats its walls with them and they are always misused. Everyone pins up anything and everything on them, placing each new piece of paper over the old ones. No one ever thinks to clear them off and after a while no one bothers to look at them any more because they are so messy and chaotic it is impossible to find anything there of value. Walking over to one, I flicked up a few sheets of yellowing paper and, sure enough, my suspicions were confirmed. Half a dozen layers down and I had already reached notices from the mid-nineties.

Shaking my head, I walked over to one of the many paper-strewn side tables. I glanced up as I heard someone walk in behind me.

'Oh, hello Trevor, you're here late,' said Alan.

Alan was one of the history teachers. He was a nice enough, easy-going chap who had been at the school for some years. He'd obviously seen a few heads come and go. He seemed pretty amenable to change, though.

'Yes, lots to do, Alan,' I said briskly. 'Do you know about the stuff on these tables? How long has it been there?'

'No, not really. It's always been there as far as I can remember.'

'How long have you been here?'

'Fifteen years.'

I grimaced. It hardly seemed possible that no one had a clue what was in these piles of paper. How could anyone live like that? Reaching for a box that had been abandoned beside one of the photocopiers that lined the walls, I knelt down by the side table. The top few layers were mainly made up of magazines and notebooks. I put them in the box, shuffling the sides to push the contents down. Alan leaned over my shoulder.

'Blimey, that stuff has been there for a while,' he commented somewhat superfluously. 'Look at the date on that. That student record is from 1985. Her kids are probably at this school by now.'

He was right. There were records going back more than a decade, nearly two in some cases. Mixed in with the pile were leaflets, fliers, textbooks and notes. I even found a bag of samples from a geography field trip. They'd all been chucked there, one after the other, and been completely forgotten about.

As I went home that evening I couldn't help reflecting, not for the first time, on the enormity of the task at Islington Green. Every time I picked up anything I seemed to uncover some new problem to be solved. Rather like those staff-room tables, there were layers upon layers of issues to sort out and tidy up.

The following morning I returned to the staff room, still pondering on what to do about it.

Looking at the tatty, ill-thought-out L-shaped room, which was now filling up with teachers, I got the impression the site had been chosen because it was as far as humanly possible away from the kids. There was a palpable and ever-present atmosphere of fear and distrust in the room. Indeed, there was more than a touch of bunker mentality among the teachers that lurked there. There were a number of noticeable cliques of teachers who would sit together in the same places each day and glare at anyone out of their immediate circle.

While any sensible person would have avoided the room at all costs, I knew I had to keep going in there to make my presence felt. Horrible, dark and filthy though it was, the teachers guarded their ownership of this room fiercely. It was definitely their domain.

That morning a pretty blond teacher whom I couldn't recall seeing before confronted me.

'Who are you?' she demanded, looking cross.

A little taken aback, I pondered on my response.

'Perhaps more to the point, I should be asking, "Who are you?"' I said. 'I am Trevor Averre-Beeson, the new head teacher.'

'Well hello,' she grinned. She was completely unfazed. 'Jane Fielding.'

Now I remembered. John Challenor had mentioned Jane a few weeks back. We were short of an English teacher and he had recommended Jane, who had worked at the school before she'd gone travelling to Australia.

'Is she any good?' I had asked.

'Yes, very good. And she can control the kids.'

'Great, then we'd better get her in.'

Jane was certainly pretty assertive. However, her reaction to me did typify the attitude of staff when they encountered me in 'their' staff room. They didn't like seeing me in there.

It seemed to me I had a number of tasks here. Firstly, I needed to modernise the staff room and create a better, more welcoming environment where the staff could relax in comfort and do work if they wanted to. I had to make it special enough that they would keep it tidy and respect the area, so we didn't end up with more piles of out-dated paperwork. Secondly, I had to relocate it so it was an appropriate size and felt like it was part of the school rather than a refuge. I had to sprinkle a bit of head-teacher love dust and use the environment to transform the 'them and us' mentality.

Previous experiences had taught me I had better tread carefully. When I announced I was refurbishing the staff room at Mayfield, the staff actually demanded a vote on whether they'd allow it to go ahead. Some of the older teachers were incensed that I had the temerity to suggest replacing their grubby old sofas with comfy new chairs. The desire for change won the day, but it taught me another valuable lesson. I had to take things one step at a time.

Amazingly, considering their reticence elsewhere, the Islington Green team welcomed the plans when I raised the idea of the new staff-room design at the staff meeting. They liked the café-style concept that I outlined, which combined high and low tables. There was noticeable excitement about the new hot-desk arrangement, with computers available to all at workstations around the room. This was in the days before laptops, so they could see this would make their lives a lot easier.

The initiative that got the biggest approval was the appointment of a member of staff to keep the room clean *and* to serve tea, coffee and biscuits at break time. I had a bit of a bust-up with the bursar over that one. He insisted we weren't allowed to do this because incentives needed to be taxed. He was also worried about the extra cost.

'Don't be ridiculous,' I said. 'It's only going to cost a few thousand pounds, and it if means that the team is focussed on the day ahead before they leave home rather than struggling to make flasks of coffee, I'll be much happier. As for the tax man, I hardly think he is worried about a few cappuccinos.'

While the staff room was being refurbished, I took the opportunity to move the exclusion room. In the early days, we had placed it on the ground floor in a position quite close to where the kids came in and out of the school building. I quickly realised this was a big mistake. It is very difficult to manage volatile children when they know their peers are just on the other side of the door. We needed to put the exclusion room in an adult part of the school, which might serve to intimidate the children into better behaviour or at the very least cut out the possibility of them showing off to the other kids. We moved the exclusion room next door to the staff room at the end of a corridor that was not usually accessible to any children at all. To get to it, children had to almost come through the staff room itself. It had the incredible effect of instantly settling most of the children who were taken to the exclusion room, which made the job of keeping them there much easier.

Location notwithstanding, I suspected that part of the reason why the exclusion room hadn't immediately worked as well at Islington Green as it had at Mayfield was because of the way it was manned. At Mayfield, Neil Ashmore, the assistant head and a formidable character, had taken charge. The children knew not to cross him. His reputation certainly preceded him. He'd been at the school for years and had been there in the days when caning was regularly used as a means of punishment and control. Neil's signature featured prominently throughout the old punishment book and there was no doubt news of his old exploits were handed down from generation to generation. If he asked for quiet, he would get it. Neil was very prescriptive in the way he wanted to run the exclusion room at Mayfield and, sensing he was exactly what it needed, I let him get on with it. He set up a series of uncompromising rules. If children spoke out of turn, they would spend another minute in there. If they did it again, they would get another half hour. He was meticulous about getting each head of department to provide age- and level-appropriate work for each year group, so not a minute of time in the exclusion room was wasted. Children would go in and study their subject and at the end of their exclusion period their work would be collected in and marked. It worked like clockwork for the school and even some of the more disruptive kids liked it. They got more study done than they ever had before and what's more they were praised and noted for it. It took a while, and a lot of trial and error, to get the exclusion room to this level at Islington Green. A lot of this was down to the fact we didn't have a character like Neil forcing it through, so I asked Marek to take charge of the facility. He had the same no-nonsense determination as Neil and the exclusion room did evolve into a successful unit over time.

Many of the most tangible problems that needed solving at Islington Green were the result of institutionalised indifference. The piles of forgotten textbooks on the staff-room table were just one small example of things being the way they were because they had been ever thus. No one could remember when they had first started, but after a while they became part of the environment. It never occurred to anyone to say, 'Hey this looks really bad,' or 'Why can't we ever find anything?' They just grumbled a little and then lived with it.

The school bell was a problem in a similar vein, although in my mind it was far more serious than the piles of paper littering side tables. When I started at Islington Green, the bell was rung no fewer than seventeen times a day. It was rung five times in the morning before the kids even arrived.

'What are they all for?' I asked John Challenor.

'Well, one of them is a warning bell to say school is going to start soon,' he began, listing them off on his fingers as he talked. 'One signals the start of assembly, except we don't actually have assembly at that time any more. Then there is the one that signals the end of the assembly we no longer have.'

I stared at John open mouthed. This was the most ludicrous thing I had heard at this school to date, against a tough field of competition. Those wretched bells were driving me nuts and I had only been in the school a short while. Moreover, they were completely useless. Apart from anything else, the idea that any organisation needs a bell to get people from place to place in this day and age when everyone has watches and phones is bizarre.

I've always been quick to get rid of bells in my previous schools. I've never seen the point of them. The analogy I'd use is that it is like when pub landlords used to call 'time' at 11pm, in the days before twenty-four-hour drinking. They'd ring the bar bell hard and everyone would ignore it and carry on merrily supping away. It wouldn't be until the landlord himself used to wander around the tables and say 'time, ladies and gents, let's be on your way' that people ever got up to leave.

'Well, let's get them switched off,' I said to John.

For some reason, against my own better judgement, I let them keep the bells that signalled the end of break time. Again, as far back as anyone could remember, the school bell had been rung to summon the children into their lessons after morning and afternoon breaks. At some point, this had clearly been deemed not quite effective enough, so teachers had been issued with small hand bells too. At the end of each break a number of teachers would be dispatched into the courtyard frantically shaking the bells to indicate they were serious: lessons were about to begin.

The children completely ignored them.

Indeed, as I discovered, classes routinely started ten

or fifteen minutes late as the teachers waited for the last stragglers to wander in. Very often, the only way to clear the courtyard was to go out there and shout 'come lads, time to go in' and then usher the children towards the entrances.

I suspected that this might partly be a bit of a happy conspiracy between staff and children. The kids would all be ten minutes late because they knew the teachers wouldn't be in their classrooms. The teachers wouldn't be in their classrooms because they knew the children would always be late. It was an ever-expanding problem and was only going to get worse. Although, of course, when the bell signalled that lessons were over, you wouldn't see the children for dust.

The team assured me that they had tried to solve the problem but hadn't had any luck. Angela Gartland, my deputy, had developed a monolithic system of recording all lateness and when the late marks accumulated to a certain level the children would get a letter home and a detention. Unfortunately the worst offenders were regularly so late that they would have ended up in detention all year if the penalties were ever properly enforced and so the system continued to fall apart. It seemed to me this was a problem that would certainly benefit from some intelligent discipline. Carrot not stick was the way to get kids to lessons on time.

Perhaps predictably, though, I faced fierce opposition from the staff at Islington Green when I brokered the idea of killing the bell altogether. I'm sure they didn't oppose every change I wanted to make on principle, but in those early days it did sometimes feel like it. Angela was particularly insistent the bells worked, even though all the available evidence appeared to point to the contrary.

I liked Angela from the beginning. She was a striking-looking woman with short, spikey blond hair, a quick wit and a quicker turn of phrase. If she didn't approve, she'd let you know. She'd come to the teaching profession late, having begun her career in the record industry, and, as such, brought a refreshing viewpoint to the job. She was also relentless. If something had to be done, I'd often defer to her. If, for example, I needed to sort out a teacher who was out of line, she would always be the first person I'd call in. She'd say, 'Leave it to me,' and that would be the last I would hear about it. Job done. Angela also wasn't one to protest for the sake of it, so I always gave her a good hearing. On the bells, though, I was convinced there must be a better way.

It so happened that, at the same time I was thinking on the bells, we began work with my old colleague and teaching consultant, John Bayley, who was doing a series of videos for Teachers TV. I had first met him some years earlier when he trained the Alec Hunter teachers in the techniques of assertive discipline. I decided to charge him with the task of coming up with a better solution to the bell issue.

'In my mind the school bell system is completely ineffective,' I told him. 'We need to find a way to persuade both the kids and my sceptical team not to rely on the bell.'

John accepted the task and over a few days observed just how ineffective the bell had become. By his reckoning, using the bells it took a *minimum* of twelve minutes for the kids to return to class. Then, after getting together a working group of teachers, including Angela, he sat down to discuss alternatives to the useless bell system. I'd already suggested that the most effective way to get things moving on time would be to simply tell the kids break was over and he agreed with me. A bit of gentle persuasion would be just as, if not more, effective that shaking bells at the children.

'I think we can refine it a little too,' John said when he reported back. 'We need to give the kids some visual clues. There are not nearly enough clocks around the place. How are they supposed to know that it is time to come in?

'In fact, we should involve them much more in this. How about enlisting their creative help to get them to draw up posters to put up around school, reminding everyone to be on time to lessons?'

We agreed on a plan where, five minutes before the end of break, a team of teachers would walk around the playground and tell children that it was time to go inside. As part of the plan to include the children more, John suggested that prefects should join the teachers to usher the children in. To help both the prefects and the staff over their fears the children would simply ignore them, or worse still fight back in some way, John organised a training session the day before we kicked off the initiative.

'We need to think about the language we use, so no one gets into a debate with the children over the bells, or lack of them,' he told the assembled teachers and prefects. 'When you say, "It is time to go in," it is inevitable that someone will ask, "Why are we doing it like this?" Don't start trying to answer with a full explanation, because you will get involved in a lengthy exchange and before you know it everyone will be as late as before. Just say, "We are doing it this way now – the bells are retired. It's time to go in."'

I was curious about how the bells' retirement would go but at the same time felt confident we were moving in the right direction. The following day, we were out in the playground in force and five minutes before the end of break we began to ask the children to go inside. Amazingly, after minimal backchat, they complied. It worked like a dream. Children were on time to lessons and at a stroke we gained a few more hours of valuable teaching time each week. It went on working too. Many weeks after John Bayley and his team packed up and left, having completed a video of the experiment, which they titled the 'No Bell Prize,' the children were still turning up to lessons on time.

Encouraged by my success with the bells, I decided to tackle another source of lateness. One of the biggest problems caused by Islington Green's seven-storey layout was that some children had to climb six staircases to get to lessons. The potential for distractions and lateness was endless.

At the next meeting of the SLT, I voiced an idea that I had been toying with for a little while.

'There are two industrial-sized lifts here, which at the moment are only used by caretakers and children that have fallen ill,' I began. 'Surely that is crazy! According to the notice on the side of the lift, they have capacity for fifty people. Why does everyone complain about using the stairs when we have two perfectly good passenger lifts? Does anyone know why they aren't used?'

No one could remember any good reason. Indeed, the SLT readily agreed it would be a good idea to use the lifts. I noticed around this time that the SLT was now generally supportive of pretty much everything I suggested, after their earlier reticence. For a few moments I wondered whether this was a good thing, but I didn't dwell on it.

The following morning I made an announcement at assembly that we would be using the lifts from now on. A cheer went up from the children and they didn't stop cheering for a full eight minutes. It was, without a doubt, the most successful assembly I had ever held.

'It will be very disciplined,' I warned them. 'There will be strict rotas and if anyone abuses the system it is back to the stairs.'

That morning the queue of children waiting to use the lifts snaked back around the ground floor. It took forty-two minutes to get the final child into their class and I had my answer to why we didn't use the lifts.

'We've evaluated the new lift policy and, after giving it serious thought, I have decided we won't be using the lifts any longer,' I said at the staff briefing the following morning, to peals of laughter all round. 'OK, OK, it was a mistake.'

Clearly not every initiative went smoothly in those early days, but, as I worked my way through my 100-day plan, there was a clear sense the school felt calmer and less manic. Both staff and children could see things were changing and for the most part they were changing for the better.

As with the lifts, though, it was still a case of a certain amount of trial and error, and even successful initiatives such as the corridor of power were not entirely fool proof. One afternoon, while I was labouring over one of the many pieces of paperwork that filled my time, my door burst open and Jason, a Year 10 student, burst into my office. He looked flushed and was even panting slightly with the exertion of the intrusion. As I looked at him he seemed to check himself, as though unsure of what to do next. Then, with a defiant look, he plonked himself down on one of the guest chairs in the centre of the room.

'Hello Jason,' I said calmly.

'Hello sir,' he said, fixing his expression into one that he supposed portrayed aggression and hostility.

'I'll be with you in just a moment,' I said, turning back to my PC, keeping my movements slow and casual.

Picking up where I left off, I carried on with my document. I sensed the atmosphere in the room shift as Jason clearly began to wonder what to do next. As the clock ticked on, he very obviously began to feel a little foolish.

After a few more minutes there was a knock at my door and Anne walked in.

'Trevor, do you realise there is a boy sitting in your chair?' she said, tentatively.

'Yes, I know, I am going to deal with him in a minute,' I said, barely looking up. 'I've just got to finish this.'

I heard the door shut as Anne slipped out. I didn't catch the expression on her face but guessed she would be pretty bemused. I carried on typing and could hear Jason beginning to shift awkwardly in his seat. After five more minutes I turned to face him.

'Now, Jason, how can I help?' I smiled.

'Er, it's nothing, sir,' he said, the expression of defiance replaced by one of sheer embarrassment.

'So you have run into the head's office after bursting through the barriers of security on the corridor, just to have a little sit and watch me writing some letters? Are you sure there is nothing you want to discuss?'

By now Jason was positively sheepish. 'No, sorry sir. I am so sorry.'

'No problem, Jason. Off you go.'

Jason hurried out of the office and within moments Angela came in. Her hand was clasped over her mouth and she was almost crying with laughter. It turned out that a bunch of the team had been in stitches outside my office. Jason had run out of Angela's room, where he was being told off for some behavioural infringement. Full of bluff and bravado, he had declared that he was going to see the head.

'How did you get him to calm down so quickly?' she laughed. 'We were all wondering what was going on in there.'

'By doing nothing,' I said.

On the way home that night, as I passed the many statues dotted around the borough of Islington, all of them looking still, purposeful and statesmanlike, I reflected on how often doing nothing is actually the right thing to do. If you wait for the moment to pass, one of two things usually happens. Either the event moves on or ceases to be a problem, or someone will come up with a good solution.

Just the day before, a huge fight had erupted right outside the school and there was a gathering of what seemed like several hundred kids. Not only was it a daunting, even terrifying, sight but it was also a potentially real public order issue. As I stood looking at the scene before me, my mind reeling about where to begin, Angela walked up to my side.

'Are you thinking what I'm thinking, Trevor?' she asked.

'I don't know. What are you thinking?' I replied, never once taking my eyes off the scene in front of us.

'That we should go inside, lock the gates and call the police.'

'I think that is exactly what we should do,' I nodded.

Angela ran off yelling instructions to the team.

'The head says lock the gates and call the police…'

There really was never a dull moment at Islington Green.

Chapter five

THE POWER
OF EFFECTIVE
COMMUNICATIONS
---

*W*hen it comes to assemblies, there are good
communicators and bad communicators. I'd like to
think I am in the former category. If I ever needed any
clues on how *not* to do it, I certainly saw some pretty
cringe-making performances in my early career. Probably
the most memorable happened during my seven years at
Boswells School in Chelmsford. The head at the time was
a lovely chap called Mr Honiker. Communication was
clearly not his forte, though. In fact, he would do his best
to hide away in the head's office for most of the week.
He went to such lengths to avoid human contact that,
when he travelled to the one lesson he took each week,
he devised a circuitous route from his office around the

edges of the school grounds to the safe confines of the Religious Education room. The assemblies he took were beyond boring and were read in a monotone from a small exercise book, which he constantly clutched in his hand. I got the clear impression he had a series of assemblies mapped out in that book that were delivered on rotation year after year. My suspicions were confirmed when he flicked the exercise book open one day and delivered the exact same assembly he had done the week before. The pages had clearly become stuck together with age. The remarkable thing is, the kids didn't even notice. They had become so thoroughly disengaged with the process they switched off the moment they sat down in the main hall.

Experiences like this made me question the value of school assemblies. The teaching day is short enough as it is without taking out a large chunk of time first thing in the morning just when many children are receptive to learning. It is so easy to squander or misuse the time. With twenty minutes stretching seemingly endlessly ahead of them, many heads try to fill the time with frankly meaningless anecdotes from their own life experiences and then seek to find some allegory to give the story meaning.

My favourite example of this came from the time when I spent the morning at Islington Green as part of the interview process. I was given the opportunity of watching the previous head, the flamboyant Marion Parsons, in action at assembly. Back then an Islington Green assembly was an extraordinary experience. It was certainly unlike any assembly I had ever witnessed before. The children's entrance into the hall was utterly chaotic as they elbowed their way through various side doors, clambered over chairs and pushed and jostled for position. I half expected them to shimmy down ropes from the ceiling. To my amazement I saw deputies desperately using loudhailers to call kids to attention, which the youngsters were managing to ignore completely despite their ear-splitting pitch.

By the time Marion swept to centre stage, the hubbub had died down to a low murmur, which I guessed was about the best she was going to get.

'Children, children,' she began, waving her hands up and down. Without pausing, she plunged on. 'I was out driving with my husband over the weekend. We were in the country and we were having a lovely day.'

I looked over at the children, whose faces were registering a range of emotions from disbelief to downright indifference.

'It was such a lovely day,' she continued, unabashed. 'On the way home, though, we ran over an animal. It was a vole. It was completely flattened, squashed onto the road.'

A few of the older boys looked up, showing a mild interest.

'I was so upset to see this poor, wretched, flattened vole, squashed onto the road, and then I thought of all of you here at Islington Green. We're all poor, wretched, flattened animals but we can't let that happen. We have to get up out of the dirt and come to life.'

Some of the children were beginning to giggle and others were looking at their friends and shaking their heads with incredulity. It was comedy central, but in a diabolical way. This place is madness on a stick, I thought.

Sorting out assemblies was definitely a point on my 100-day plan but I wasn't about to do away with them. From initially doubting the point of having them at all, I had over my career grown to value them. Indeed, I saw them as an opportunity to nurture and promote all the other work being done to transform a school and in particular to communicate a positive message of hope. In short, assemblies, handled correctly, can make an important contribution. Luckily, I was under no illusion that it would be an easy job, as I discovered at my very first assembly.

I opted to set out my stall at that assembly with a message that would resonate with the children and hopefully make them sit up and take notice. The children clearly saw it as a badge of some considerable pride that the school had had such considerable involvement in Pink Floyd's album *The Wall*. The famous chorus 'we don't need no education!' was regularly chanted as they milled around the corridors, even though the kids who had originally sung on the album had long since grown up.

I decided to break the ice with my new charges by referring to the song. I reasoned I might create an instant rapport by mentioning it and showing it in a positive light.

'I am very aware of the school's past involvement with Pink Floyd and its contribution to *The Wall*,' I began, confidently addressing the sea of cynical faces in front of me. 'What I wondered though is, how many of you realise that when we say 'we don't need no education' what we are actually saying is 'we *do* need an education'. It is a double negative...'

I'd barely got to the first syllable of 'negative' before a Year 10, at the back of the hall, stood up.

'No we fucking don't,' he yelled, raising his fist.

The whole school erupted into laughter, leaving me wondering what I had let myself in for in this new job. Mentally, I raised 'sort out assemblies' a few places up the list on my growing action plan.

It occurred to me that I would never get my message of positivity across while simultaneously trying to control the whole school. I'd seen the chaos of the vole assembly with Marion, where the staff had been powerless in controlling the students even when they used loudhailers. The only option was to break the process down into manageable chunks and hold year-group assemblies. I suspected the older kids would be too set in their ways to be controlled even in the smaller crowds of their year groups, so I began to run Year 10 and Year 11 assemblies on a half-year-group basis.

My strategy for assemblies was partly inspired by the wisdom of two people. The first, the educator Sir Tim Brighouse, once said that it is wise for head teachers to spin just a little ahead of the truth. The second source was a little closer to home and was in fact my father-in-law, Colin Mitchell, a retired police inspector, who told me,

'If you are going to tell a lie, tell it to everybody.'

Clearly, as a headmaster, I can't tell lies. As John Bayley insists, there is little point saying to children that they are all going to get straight As when they are only expected to attain Cs or Ds. However, if I say they are in line for Bs, they won't be far off when they get a C and might even be inspired to better things. I never shy away from being optimistic about the truth, as far as it can realistically go. It is all part of developing the leadership narrative of a school's journey.

My assemblies at Islington Green were relentlessly positive. Instead of talking about the fight outside the school gate on Monday and delivering dire warnings to anyone planning a rematch, I aimed to tell the assembled throng at least three good things that were happening in school that week. I never, ever talked about bad things unless in the most extreme of circumstances.

Instead of meaningless 'thoughts for the week' or anecdotes about my weekend, I talked about real, concrete achievements: 'It has been a great week. Did you know, our Year 11 football team won for the ninety-ninth consecutive time?'

Every example showed the school was different now and every week a different story was told using cases from all over the school. After a while of relentlessly coming up with good stuff, something began to change. It happened slowly at first and was barely perceptible, but there was a noticeable sense of optimism in the air.

The children started to think, hey, this school isn't so bad now. We really do go to a great school.

It was not just the kids who benefited either. The unrelenting positivity began to rub off on staff too. I'll never forget the first time I overheard two teachers walking away from one of my assemblies saying to one another, 'I didn't know that was happening, did you? That's amazing.' They were right too. None of these feel-good stories would ever have come out otherwise. All anyone would have focussed on would have been the fight outside.

Over time, the trail started to loop back. Staff started seeking me out to tell me about positive stories rather than constantly berating me about one disaster after another. The confident message filtered through and people became inspired. When people are positively inspired it is possible to achieve just about anything.

Another bonus to assemblies is that, used well, they can be a brilliant nudge for teachers. This is something I discovered almost by accident while at Boswells School in the mid-eighties. I'd started there as an economics teacher, but after being promoted to head of year a couple of things changed. The first was that I was put in charge of personal social health education (PSHE) and the second was that I was charged with taking both full-year assemblies and half-year assemblies. In fact, truth be told, I didn't *have* to take on all the assemblies. However, none of the other Boswells teachers were keen, so I said I'd do them all. It didn't bother me much. Even though

I had once questioned their value, I had always rather enjoyed giving assemblies.

With quite a lot on my plate, I decided the most effective way to go forward would be to somehow combine at least some parts of my new responsibilities. I decided to make assemblies like lead lessons for what the teachers were going to do in PSHE. In my experience, most of the staff didn't take PSHE very seriously. They didn't plan for it and it was rather shoved into the background.

I spent the summer holidays planning out PSHE lessons for the following academic year, bringing together a bunch of materials and schemes of work. Everything was in place and ready to go by September. The next stage in my strategy was to use assembly to outline to the kids what they'd be doing in PSHE and at the same time train the teachers on what they were going to do. It was, I believed, an engaging way to get everyone on board.

It all appeared to go quite well and the children seemed quite enthusiastic. However, I couldn't quite shake the feeling that the teachers were not completely on board. I sensed a continuing cynicism around the whole subject and suspected the teachers would ignore my carefully-laid-out lesson plans, believing they knew much better than their youthful new head of year. Sure enough, in the coming days, I was proved right. The PSHE lessons were all over the place.

Feeling a little exasperated, I decided to give the teachers a further nudge in the right direction at the next assembly.

'This is a very exciting week for you all,' I told the assembled group of children. 'This week in PSHE you will all be learning about…'

I then laid out a very compelling view of what they would be working on in their PSHE classes. In the coming days the children didn't let it drop and would even interrupt the teacher to remind them: 'Please sir, Mr Averre-Beeson said we'd be doing presentations this week.'

It would take a very stubborn teacher indeed to ignore this sort of pressure and sure enough the staff were gradually brought into line and my carefully-set-out lesson plan was taught as intended. I introduced the technique into all my assemblies at each subsequent school, including Islington Green. I did it in a very positive way, urging the children to get excited about things like the new rewards structure or merits system that was being introduced. I figured that, if I didn't have complete enthusiasm from the kids about the benefits of good behaviour, it would be difficult to get total buy-in from teachers. Once I had told the children what we were doing, there was pressure on the team to get into line.

Without proper thought and application, assemblies can descend into the worst sort of wasted opportunity. With effective communication, however, they can be used as an powerful campaign tool in a host of different ways. The key is to be relentlessly positive and to find interesting and useful things to talk about. I found another great way to get children to engage was to make assemblies interactive. This is 100 per cent more effective than the model where one person stands at the front and yarns on for twenty minutes about nothing in particular.

I have two dead easy stock assemblies up my sleeve. The first one is based on the humble potato. In the morning, before I left for Islington Green, I picked up a handful of potatoes. I handed them out around the room in assembly and asked each of the children who got one to study the vegetable while I was talking.

'I want you to study your potato and get to know it,' I said. Then, to lighten the mood, I added something silly like, 'Imagine you are going on a date with it.'

After a while I gathered the potatoes back in and mixed them up. Putting them down on a table, I invited the children to come up to the front and retrieve their potato. They all came up and confidently picked out their own. It was a bit of a magician's trick really because sure enough whenever I did this assembly one of the potato bearers invariably took me aside later on.

'I didn't get my potato back, sir, I couldn't find my one,' the child would say conspiratorially. 'I took another one so as not to embarrass you.'

Still, the exercise held their attention brilliantly and allowed me to make some pertinent points about how, even though we are all races and creeds, we are all individuals.

Another Islington Green assembly that went down particularly well was a shameless lift from the work of the American economist Milton Friedman. I held up a pencil and asked the students to tell me how many people it had taken to make this everyday object. Younger children began their guesses in single digits and, like an auctioneer, I went around the room taking estimates. Eventually, I told them they were all wrong and that it had actually taken 599,000 people to make the pencil. Cue shocked looks all around the hall, but I had the full attention of everyone in the room. I moved on to ask them where the wood came from, where the saw was made that cut the tree down for the wood, how many people it took to make the ship that delivered the materials and so on. By taking the example of something as simple as a pencil, which we all use every day, I was able to make some interesting points about economics and basic philosophy. Most importantly, I had their full attention.

Assemblies were not the only forums through which I spread and reinforced my vision of positivity. Even though the message was gaining momentum, there was a need for a clear communications strategy throughout the school. We needed to underline the message in everything we did and said in the classroom, outside the school and in the staff room – in fact, wherever and whenever there was an opportunity. I had to get everyone to buy into the notion that it is so much more effective to be positively redirectional. Recognising the good things and constantly pointing out that a school is a great place *makes* it a great place. Spending the majority of the time telling people what you don't want them to do and what a disaster everything is simply becomes a self-fulfilling prophecy.

One of the most important areas to fix in this respect

was the significant number of staff who had clearly not yet bought into the vision. Even though things were certainly improving in other areas of the school and a number of the team had been hugely enthusiastic, every time I walked into the staff room I was constantly struck by how heavy and oppressive the atmosphere felt in there. There was still a tangible air of despair among some teachers as they recovered between lessons and, as time ticked on, many of them shot nervous glances at the clock as though they were just about to head out into the gladiatorial arena.

I realised that one thing that was certainly not helping was the regular gloom-laden announcements from Angela, the deputy head. Nearly every briefing, she would walk in, call the teachers to attention and update them on the worst things the school had to offer.

Whenever I called in to the staff room I was invariably just in time to hear her reading from her clipboard: 'I just want to tell you about incidents yesterday. There were three boys who had their heads cracked open in the playground. One was an accident and two were the result of deliberate fights. Some of you probably heard about the fight after school…'

As the endless list of negative events rolled on, I looked around at the faces of the teachers. Many of them just looked beaten down by it all. Why were they being told all this, I wondered? I speculated that many teachers might not have even been aware of the fight outside the gates. It had clearly been dealt with, so what was the value in continuing to talk about it?

Trevor Averre-Beeson's earlier parallel career fronting the band The Press, which was signed to EMI

Holding Islington Green's coveted discs celebrating its pupils' involvement in the chorus of Another Brick in the Wall. (Islington Gazette)

TES cartoon from January 2003, Islington Green had become famous for being the school Tony Blair wouldn't send his son to – now with results on the rise things looked different. (Martin Rowson)

Trevor speaking to more than 400 Lilac Sky employees at the 5th Annual Education Awards in July 2014.

The power of effective communications

Staff were being faced with negative messages everywhere they looked and most of the time these was completely unnecessary. The school bulletins that were distributed to each classroom on a daily basis, for example, listed the names of each child who had been excluded. When I joined, that was a lot of names too.

'What was the point of that?' I asked Angela when I sat down with her later on.

'Teachers need to know which children won't be coming to classes,' was the reply.

'Surely though,' I reasoned, 'the teachers in the relevant classes could be informed personally? It makes little sense to tell everyone about the exclusions and merely adds to an already poor self-image for the school.

'There was no need for the librarian, who has never even taught a class, to know about exclusions. Neither does the learning resources officer, who runs the photocopier, need to be told. Indeed, if he wasn't constantly reminded of how awful the kids all were, maybe he wouldn't be too scared to come out of his room and might even begin to move freely around the school so he could do his job properly. In fact, why does *anyone* need to know all this stuff?'

Angela nodded. 'When you put it like that,' she smiled. 'I guess we've always…'

'…done it that way?' I said, finishing her sentence. If I'd had a pound for every time I heard this phrase at Islington Green I would have been a much richer man. 'Let's drop the negative bulletins, verbal and written.'

Islington Green was doing a great job of showing

everyone how bad it was, whereas what it really needed was for a leader to stand up and tell staff, the children, parents and anyone who would listen that they were all great. After that day, gone were the endless lists of exclusions in the school bulletins, and breathless announcements of bad behaviour were banned in the staff room. This had an almost instant effect. Indeed, one teacher reported back to me that it was 'as though the school had suddenly become a better place overnight'. Nothing had really changed, but we had stopped dwelling on all the bad stuff.

Of course it was always the 'big' stories that motivated the children most and guaranteed their full attention. Being sited in central London, Islington Green was constantly in demand for filming for this or that and, as I was always welcoming of such opportunities, the film companies kept coming back. I did it for two reasons. Firstly, a few days filming usually guaranteed a much-needed cash injection to the school fund and, secondly, it motivated the children. Telling them at assembly about the school's role in a documentary or film project always made them sit up and take notice. While I had their full attention I could invariably slip in a few subliminal positive messages too.

One event that caused the biggest stir was our work with celebrity chef Jamie Oliver. Jamie was at the peak of his fame, having done three series of *The Naked Chef* for the BBC and having been the face of Sainsbury's since the millennium. He was just setting out on his healthy eating for schools campaign and his production team asked me whether Islington Green would be willing to play host to the chef. I agreed straight away and for the next few weeks our school kitchens were a whirl of activity. Although Jamie's programmes were to be recorded 'live', there was a lot of pre-prep that went on, not least to discover the various characters to be found in the school kitchen.

It just so happened that the show coincided with the final days of Andy Gollifer's initial refurbishment project at Islington Green. After sorting out the entrances and staff areas, Andy had gone on to oversee a complete redesign of the canteen, which had previously been one of the most awful parts of the whole school. The performing-arts area had had a complete overhaul too, which was important because performing arts was central in the culture of the school. Not only did Islington Green have Pink Floyd in its heritage but it also had a long tradition of music and drama, which I wanted to promote. The drama studios now looked lovely and had proper sprung flooring.

A thought occurred to me that it would be a great boost to all concerned if Jamie Oliver would come along to preside over some sort of official opening ceremony. It would demonstrate a positive seal of approval for all our hard work and deliver the message in the best possible way to appeal to the kids. I didn't really see how Jamie could refuse; after all, we had already gone to a great deal of trouble for his programme.

I rang the production team, whom I had got to

know quite well, and asked whether there was any chance of Jamie doing the honours.

'Well, we're not his bosses, but you've done a lot for us, so I'm sure he'll be amenable,' came the reply from the producer, an impossibly young chap called Julian. 'Let us just check it with him.'

Julian came back almost straight away and said Jamie would be very happy to do it.

A date was set and we got busy with the preparations. As expected, anybody and everybody wanted to be there. The guest list of over 200 people had to be tightly controlled. As well as a handpicked list of children and staff, we also had acceptances from the mayor, the junior Education Minister Stephen Twigg, various local dignitaries and a number of print and TV journalists. As the day approached there was a palpable sense of excitement among both the children and staff.

A few weeks before the event there was a slightly heart-stopping moment when Julian called to tell us rather apologetically that they wouldn't be filming with us after all. They had decided to go with Kidbrooke School in Greenwich.

'He will still be coming to our opening, won't he?' I asked, somewhat nervously.

'Oh, yes, yes, it's in the diary, don't worry about that,' Julian said confidently.

That was a relief. I couldn't imagine having to unravel all the preparations.

Then, just twenty-four hours before the launch, I

received an unexpected call. Julian sounded crestfallen.

'Trevor, I am really sorry about this, but I am afraid Jamie is unable to make it. His filming schedule has run over and there is no way he can make it across town.'

For a few seconds I was speechless. We had been immersed in the excitement of this big celebrity launch for weeks now and in an instant it had all come crashing down around my ears.

'But we've got the world and his wife coming,' I managed to say at last.

'Well, he never absolutely promised he would come and you know what it's like.'

I could hardly believe what Julian was saying. He must have realised what a disappointment this would be to everyone.

'No, I'm not sure that I do,' I said, doing my best to sound calm. 'You said it was in the diary. I can't see how we can let everyone down.'

'Look, I know it looks bad, but there is nothing we can do about it. Jamie himself is really apologetic. He's going to send over one of his fifteen chefs and a whole load of signed books…'

I let Julian's words wash over me. I had no idea how I would possibly begin to unpick everything just twenty-four hours before the launch. In fact, I was so distressed by the turn of events, I couldn't bring myself to break it to anyone that day. I let them all carry on with the arrangements in blissful ignorance.

I didn't sleep much that night and the following day I

still had no idea what to do. For a few brief moments I even considered calling in sick. Eventually, with a heavy heart, I went into school, gathered up the senior team and broke the news: Jamie wasn't coming. There were gasps of shock and disbelief, but seeing their reaction helped galvanise me into doing something about our terrible position.

'Keep this to yourselves,' I commanded. 'Carry on as before. I've got an idea.'

When the time came and I made the announcement to the crowd assembled for the event that the Naked Chef would not be joining us, there was a predictable roar of disappointment. However, Stephen Twigg very gamely stepped into the breach and did the honours. In fact, he did a fantastic impersonation of Jamie Oliver and really turned things around. Everyone there rallied and the evening was an unexpected success.

There were a lot of journalists there that evening and the press write-ups noted Jamie Oliver's absence and questioned the wisdom of letting down a school during Oliver's high-profile campaign to raise standards for children. His press spokesperson responded with the line that he had never actually promised to be there and his appearance was always subject to his filming schedule. Word got back to us that Oliver and his team were a bit irritated by the whole thing, particularly the implication he had let us down. It is not for me to say either way now. I am just pleased that we managed to turn the event around and that it ended in a positive way for the team.

Chapter six

A VISION OF CALM

Most of us, if we are honest with ourselves, know our own failings. How we then deal with them is peculiar to each one of us. Some people expend a lot of time and energy trying to hide them, or in making sure they don't get found out, while others very sensibly look for ways to shore up their own failings.

I like to think I fall into the latter category. As I prepared to take on my first headship, at Mayfield School in London's Redbridge, Hugh Richie, the head from Alec Hunter, my previous school, took it upon himself to give me some words of advice. Back then, as an ambitious young man in my mid-thirties, I thought he was a sage old chap so I had better take note. Now I realise he was actually a rather sprightly fifty-year-old, but that is by the by. He said that I should always be myself and I should start the way I meant to go on. It was his third piece of advice, though, that I took most to heart. He pointed out that, while I had many strengths, I wasn't so hot on the nitty-gritty of compiling data.

'Make sure you have someone who is good on that,' he warned.

I had to agree with his assessment and have probably over-compensated ever since. I have also, over time, become much more patient with the failings of those around me. This is, I am told, quite unusual. Those in a position of power are often utterly amazed when someone below them makes a big mistake.

'How could you possibly have overlooked that?' they will explode, when the mistake is discovered. Or: 'I was perfectly clear in my instructions. Why couldn't you do what you were asked?'

Leaders frequently expect everyone to work in a perfect, robotic way and, when they don't, demonstrating their weaknesses, the leaders act surprised. They refuse to accept the failings of others. In truth what we should be doing is accepting everyone has weakness, recognising them and then planning for weakness and fallibility.

When I started at Mayfield, not long after hearing Richie's wise words, it felt pretty good. I can't deny I relished the thought of being in charge and fully able to put my own plans into practice. I was keen to stamp my mark straight away and made a number of immediate policy changes. A fairly minor one was that I expected every teacher to return their class data by lunchtime on Friday. Come Friday I was shocked to discover that, out of eighty teachers, only nineteen had returned their class data by midday. I couldn't understand the problem. It certainly didn't seem a difficult thing to do.

It festered away in my mind over the whole weekend and on Monday morning I didn't hold back in berating all the teachers who had failed in this seemingly simple task. Looking around at the look of surprise on the assembled faces, I was sure my sharp words had done the trick. I waited for the remaining class data to flood in.

By the end of that week only a further nineteen reports had trickled in. This would be trickier than I thought, I mused, before asking Brenda, my PA, to send out a memo to remind the stragglers. The memo only managed to elicit a handful of responses. I upped the ante by sending out a memo printed on red paper, aping the red reminder letters so loved by utility companies. Nothing.

Finally, at my wits' end, I said to Brenda, 'Will you go around and see those idiots who haven't given in their class data and ask for it?'

I still only made it to a 95 per cent response rate even after this direct intervention.

I realised then there was little point in following this routine every time I asked for any sort of data. Issuing edits, sanctions and threats wasn't doing much good and the only real concrete outcome was mounting frustration for me.

I thought back to my conversation with Richie about failings and realised I had to plan for the weaknesses of my team, accept them and work with them. All too often, I hear heads say what a stressful and lonely job theirs is. The reason they are stressed is they are expecting themselves to be perfect and they are expecting other people to be perfect too. As soon as they relax and say, 'I am not perfect, but I don't expect my team to be perfect either,' they'll be able to focus on doing the things they can do as well as is practically possible.

Once I had understood and accepted where the weaknesses lay in my team at Mayfield, I had to find a way to subtly nudge them into doing what I wanted. I set in place an event on the fourth Friday of every month where I invited everyone in for a free pizza. Then, while they were munching away on their margaritas, I'd tell them they had to write out their data while I was still in the room. One or two of them snuck out without giving me any data, but I got what I wanted in the main part.

Operating on the expectation of weakness is far more effective (and less stressful) than operating on the expectation of strength.

I was reminded of this when I joined Islington Green. The team had been through a pretty torrid few years. Before I arrived, morale had sunk to an all-time low, dozens of teachers had left and those that remained had faced change after change, with very few having a positive effect. Indeed, it seemed that, whatever happened, the results kept sinking.

There have been a number of academic studies on how employees react to change. Apparently, my experience at Islington Green is not unusual. To begin with, a team will become angry and resentful about what will be needed to make the required changes happen and may even feel demoralised and depressed. They will then move into a bargaining stance where they will try to stamp their mark on the new regime. Finally, all being well, they will either accept the change and line up behind it or leave altogether.

As time went on, though, I was starting to feel we were firmly stuck in the demoralised and depressed phase. One of the most exhausting parts about being a head at a school like Islington Green is that it is like conducting open-heart surgery all day long. People were constantly coming into my office and saying, 'Sorry to disturb you, this is just a quick one,' and then launching into something that was anything but brief or simple. It was one thing after the other and no one seemed able to see a way beyond the problems that faced them as individuals or the school as a whole.

Everything seemed to drag the staff down. As much as I tried to flood the school with positivity, the slightest setback would pull people off track. They couldn't see through the bad things.

This was certainly the case when Janet, one of our trainee teachers, came to me.

'I can't cope,' she said, slumping into a chair, looking completely exhausted.

'What with?' I asked. I was a bit taken off guard because we hadn't really spoken much yet.

'Everything,' she replied, and it was obvious from her face that she wasn't kidding.

I got up from the seat behind my desk and sat down

in a chair across from her. Whatever else I had on at that moment would have to wait.

'Can you tell me a bit more, so I can see if I can help?' I said.

Janet didn't hold back. She'd clearly been waiting to be asked and now she wasn't going to lose the opportunity. She told me she couldn't cope with all the paperwork she'd been getting as a trainee teacher, she couldn't cope with the kids, she couldn't cope with her line managers, her parents, her boyfriend – the list went on. The facts of the matter were she couldn't cope with anything.

As she ran through the list, I mentally weighed up my options. The most obvious response would have been to gently ask why she didn't look for another job. But I didn't.

Instead, I said, 'Why don't you go home and take some time out to think about whether you are doing the right thing working here? Then, next week, why don't you just come in for the bits of the job you find OK and we will cover you for the bits that aren't.

'Then, let's keep talking. I might not be the right person to talk to about your home life, but Angela, my deputy, is great on relationships and is always advising me on what I should be saying to my partner. Talk to Angela when you feel down.'

The look of relief on Janet's face was immense. It took a load off her mind that someone had listened to her. Janet did spend some time out, but she came back and over time went on to become one of our best teachers. Indeed, she eventually went on to become a head of year.

A vision of calm

Reflecting on my conversation with Janet, I believe a lot of the problem was down to the fact she felt she was under pressure to be perfect. It is a modern phenomenon that in our competitive world people imagine they have to be the best at everything to succeed.

As I have already said, I don't expect perfection in any of my team. I know everyone is flawed, especially me. I've done enough psychometric tests in my time to know where I am lacking and, for the record, the quadrant of my brain that doesn't work as well as the other three is the one that governs vertical filing skills. Apparently, I am not the best person to entrust with putting things into alphabetical order or remembering where things have been left.

Based on my own results, I know that my colleagues will each have one area (or perhaps more) that isn't as strong as the others and I am prepared for it. As long I'm aware of this, I can work to put members of my team in the right places to suit their abilities. Whenever I am considering a new teacher, I am never side-tracked by looking for an individual who is 100 per cent right for the position, with exactly the right attitude and achievements. That perfect person doesn't exist. I positively recognise the things they can do well and remain aware of the bits they aren't so good at. I am realistic in the selection of my teams and, while I pay attention to their qualifications, experience and achievements, I also look closely at their psychology, motivations and behaviour. By accepting that they are not 100 per cent at everything and capitalising on their strengths, I build up their loyalty. They know I am not going to decimate their career because they are not good at one thing, and that can prove to be hugely motivational.

By the same token, I've never understood leaders who get rid of perfectly good people because they are not brilliant at every aspect of their job. So they are rubbish with finances? Well, don't let them loose on the books. If you sack them, you will get rid of someone who has perfectly decent strengths elsewhere.

Similarly, the last thing I want is for anyone to *pretend* they are perfect. Whenever anyone pretends they are perfect at something, problems get stacked up in a drawer somewhere waiting for someone else to find them.

The experience with Janet stiffened my resolve to do more to build up and motivate the team at Islington Green. It has long been my assertion that, while many leaders pay lip service to the fact their team is their greatest asset, not enough do anything concrete to protect that asset or better still help it grow in value.

Popular leadership thought often says it is only group performance that matters. People need to work closely together as a team for the group to be effective. This is all about the belief that 'we can do it' is stronger than an individual's belief that 'I can do it.' I agree with this philosophy up to a point. However, I also believe that, in a people-orientated sector like ours, managing the strengths and expectations of individuals has a vital part to play in ensuring their motivation and efficacy.

Being a leader should never mean that you are too

lofty to be concerned about the little things individual members of your team do that make a big difference. However important you are (or think you are), you should never forget to praise and thank people for a job well done.

I instigated a system where every week, at the key strategic meeting of senior staff, I asked the team to recommend someone who had done something worth recognition. I called this a 'quality circle'. It didn't matter whether the person being singled out was a head of year, a teacher or a cleaner. It didn't have to take too much effort either. All I needed was a name and a sentence about what the person had done. Perhaps it was a teaching assistant who had helped a child who broke their arm, spending the evening with them in casualty until their parents arrived. Or a teacher who routinely organised an annual trip for kids. It might even have been someone who had demonstrated the smallest act of initiative, such as clearing out the stock cupboard. Each one of these selfless acts contributed to the smooth running of the school and undoubtedly deserved recognition.

I sent thank-you letters to each of the people who were nominated, which was no small undertaking. Within a short space of time there were up to thirty nominations a week. Occasionally people would ask me whether it was worth it and I always encouraged the questioner to look at the scheme from their own point of view. How good does it feel to be recognised for going the extra mile or above and beyond? It also shows that, while I am a busy person, I am prepared to make time for the people who are important. That is a powerful message to staff.

Ideas like the quality circle had many other virtues too. As the head, I started to hear about the many thoughtful acts I might otherwise have known nothing about. People at Islington Green were always quick to tell me about things that had gone wrong, but the good things? They didn't filter through until I actively invited people to tell their stories.

There was a little resistance to the idea at first. Staff took time to warm up to it and may even have been a little cynical. Indeed, Ken Muller even came right out and said it was nonsense.

'Paula is just doing her job. Why should we reward that over and above the recognition everyone else is getting?' he said. 'Why are you bothered about this?'

Over time, though, a momentum began to build and the majority of the staff welcomed the fact their efforts were finally being recognised. After years of being told how rubbish they all were, it made a nice change for someone to turn around and say, 'Well done – you are doing a good job.'

As the team became more amenable to praise and the personal touch, I extended the idea to make sure I always gave a birthday card to everyone who worked in the school. In a school with upwards of 150 staff, this was quite a commitment, but a small gesture like this can make a remarkable difference to morale. It was a subtle way of recognising people and showing they were part of a team. With a little organisation it wasn't too onerous either. I learned to keep a good stock of cards and Anne was ruthlessly efficient with her diary of all the dates. It didn't take a minute to write something along the lines of 'Simon, I loved the Year 8 interpretation of *Oliver*. Thanks for all your work on that. Have a great birthday.'

Of course, there were still the odd pockets of resistance at Islington Green. The old die-hards who would complain about pretty much anything. Sure enough, a birthday card to one of the teachers was handed back to Anne with a rather curt message. The cutting rebuke went along the lines that I was behaving like a lord of the manor, handing out pennies to his serfs. The person in question did have some serious personality issues, though, so I didn't take the rebuff too badly.

If I was honest, though, it was often tough trying to get my vision across to the team and to motivate them enough to help me realise it. I felt like I was constantly fire fighting and there were still some staff who seemed indifferent to my efforts however far I went. I needed a sign that we were finally getting somewhere to prove all the positivity I had been banging on about was indeed having an effect. The answer, when it arrived, came from two sources: the 'wanderers' and my first Ofsted inspection at Islington Green.

First the wanderers. On almost my first day at Islington Green I had received a list from Theo, one of the admin team. He simply walked into my office, because these were the days when I still had multiple entrances, plonked the list down and left without offering an explanation. This became a fairly regular routine.

'What is this list?' I asked John at the next SLT meeting.

Taking the list, John surveyed the names.

'They are the wanderers,' he said, handing it back.

'The wanderers? Are they a football team?'

John laughed. 'No, they are the kids who are found outside in the corridors.'

'But there must be, what, ninety names on this list! What do we do with them once they are ticked off on the list? Take them back? What?'

'Well, there is little point taking them back to the classrooms. The teachers won't take them if they have missed the beginning of the lesson and they probably wouldn't stay anyhow.'

'So what is the point of the list?'

'Historically, I believe it was so the school could note them on the registration system and keep the numbers up.'

Great, I thought, another massive problem to solve. A quick survey found there were around 100 habitual wanderers. Most of them had special educational needs and nearly all had emotional and behavioural difficulties. As there was no real special needs provision for them, they simply dropped out of the system and hung around the corridors, or around the back of the gym. They might pop into the PE class if they fancied it, but other than that lessons were out. It was pretty self-evident this state of affairs couldn't continue. I'd only been at the school a short time, but it was inevitable that we'd be inspected at some point in the near future. If we didn't sort out the wanderers we'd never stand a chance of getting out of the 'serious weaknesses' category.

I thought back to one of my first jobs, as a teacher at Boswells School near Chelmsford, where I taught economics and psychology. To balance my timetable they gave me the naughty kids, who all had emotional and behavioural difficulties. I had them for fifteen periods every week and had to think up interesting projects to occupy them. Before long I became pretty inventive. We did work about the music business, we looked at excavated Roman ruins – all sorts. I introduced a scoring system and said that all those who got over ten behavioural points each week (which was strangely all of them) would go on a trip. Every Friday I'd pile them into the school minibus and take them to the local country park for a fifteen-minute run around. They loved it and I would get a precious few minutes sitting in the sun reading a paper. Everyone was happy. I introduced something similar at both Alec Hunter and Mayfield and it worked very well for the dozen or so kids who needed extra attention. The problem I had at Islington Green was that there were not just a dozen of these kids. At this school, there were nearly 100. It was tricky.

After giving the matter some further thought, I came up with the idea of a referral unit for the really difficult children, which I called the Learning Zone. It would be set up in an old Victorian building that was slightly separate to the main school. Working once again with

Andy Gollifer, we designed a comfortable and inviting space that we filled with comfy sofas and beanbags, computers and learning games. It even had a beautifully landscaped roof garden. I decided we could get away with operating the Learning Zone on a shift system, so we could have thirty children in there during the morning, from 9am to 1pm, and thirty from 1pm to 5pm. It would be staffed by the existing special needs teachers, who were at that time dotted around the school, at a ratio of one teacher to three children.

While the rooms were being refurbished and set up, we had to decide which children we would send there. I decided that any child who was referred to the exclusion room more than twelve times might be considered, but other than that we didn't really have a proper way of assessing how much special needs provision was required in the school.

At Islington Green, in the past one of the deputies used to stand up in assembly and say, 'All the children who have learning difficulties and can't read properly, can you put your hands up? Very good. Go and see Mr Bashir, the special needs coordinator.'

Clearly this wasn't an option. Instead, I asked the staff to write down the names of the five most difficult and challenging children in their class – children whom they believed had learning needs and who might be candidates for the Learning Zone. I asked them to state exactly why they had made each choice. They all completed this task and Angela and John sifted through the dozens of lists, which flooded in with surprising speed. We picked out the seventy names that appeared the most and these were the first children to enter the Learning Zone, in January 2003.

These children loved it. Suddenly they felt safe and had somewhere to go. They started late, left early and didn't have breaks with the other kids. There was a very strong rewards system that meant, at long last, the children made huge progress with their learning. Their parents loved it too because finally their sons and daughters were getting the attention they needed. The parents were called every day with a progress report.

Positive discipline was a vital element in the way we dealt with the former wanderers too. I set out very clear rules on how to speak to them and address any potential transgressions. One boy, Johnny, was a habitual smoker. He clearly believed smoking gave him kudos.

'Just deal with it in the same way as you'd deal with everything else,' I explained to the staff. 'Stay calm and say: "Johnny, you are smoking, I need you to stop. It is a warning. Put the cigarette away, there's a good lad."

'Then, walk away.'

If an adult stood over Johnny until he put out his ciggy, it would come across as a challenge and would probably quickly escalate into a battle. Instead, when I was confronted with a situation like this, I'd tell kids like Johnny that I'd be back in five minutes.

'If it is away, then we are all good,' I'd say.

If a teacher says this in a non-confrontational way and then walks away, by the time they circle back a few minutes later the cigarette will be gone in 99 out of 100 cases. To reinforce what has just happened, I always recommend saying something like, 'Well done, Johnny. Thanks very much.'

Pretty soon, the moment any teacher spots Johnny, or indeed anyone, having a sneaky cigarette, the child will say, 'I know, I know, I have to put it away.' By adopting a more measured approach and playing on psychology rather than resorting to hostility, it was possible for us to consistently achieve better outcomes at Islington Green.

Working *with* the more difficult children, rather than existing in a state of perpetual conflict, and introducing the Learning Zone transformed the school overnight too. There was no more corridor wandering, and morale among teachers soared because they finally felt they could handle the twenty-five kids who were left in their class.

The shift in our fortunes came in the nick of time, too. Just one month after the Learning Zone was opened, the expected Ofsted inspection began. The day of the inspection did 'coincide' with the day of a school trip for half a dozen of the most challenging children in the Learning Zone. As I explained to the inspectors, the trip to North Yorkshire had been in the dairy for some time. I did offer to pay for some of the inspectors to shadow the trip, but they didn't take me up on the offer. As it turned out, it was a good thing too. A couple of the more unmanageable kids got out of control and ended up doing a significant amount of damage to a tableau at a historic site, which we had to pay for out of school funds.

Ofsted inspections are always crucial, but this one was going to be a game changer. What I hadn't realised when I accepted the job (and what no one had seen fit to mention) was that if we failed this inspection the school would have to close altogether. We were in serious weaknesses and had had several inspections already. According to the rulebook, if we slipped back into special measures it was game over. I'd be out of a job and everything I'd managed to do so far would have been for naught. It was a tense time.

Fortunately, the inspection was positive and took Islington Green out of significant weaknesses, which was a further morale boost for everyone. In those days, a school would either pass an inspection or not. There was none of the detail that has been introduced since. The inspectors did kindly describe the curriculum and teaching as 'good', which allowed us to say we had had a 'good' inspection. They also described me as 'visionary and transformational', which was very helpful indeed. It legitimised what I was doing at the school. Most importantly, for anyone who thought the things I was doing were a bit wacky or who didn't get it, the inspection proved we were going in the right direction.

Not many months after the results came in from the successful Ofsted inspection, I received a rather intriguing job application. It was from Peter Hyman, Tony Blair's speechwriter, who had played an integral part in bringing Labour to victory in 1997.

The first I knew about it was when Anne popped her

head around the door and said Number Ten was on the phone.

'Number ten what?' I replied.

'Number Ten, Number Ten,' she said, raising her eyebrows for emphasis.

'What, Downing Street?' I said, as the penny dropped, although I was still mystified.

'Yes,' she laughed. 'It's a man called Peter Hyman. He says he is the communications director.'

'Right,' I said, still confused. Then I added, as much to myself as to Anne, 'What could that be all about?'

'Maybe it is *that* call,' she said conspiratorially.

'What call?'

'You know, *that* call. A knighthood…'

'Oh, get lost. Put him through.'

Peter came on the line and quickly introduced himself. He was very well spoken and I immediately pictured a middle-aged, smartly dressed, privately educated man.

'I wondered whether I might come to see you,' he said, after the usual pleasantries. 'I have a, er, somewhat unusual proposition to put to you.'

'OK,' I said, intrigued. I honestly could not imagine what it might be. I knew better than to question him on it over the phone, though. It was clearly something he wanted to ask me to my face. It was up to me whether I was interested enough in what he had to say to invite him in on spec. I found I was.

'Why don't I put you back through to Anne and she'll put a date in the diary?' I suggested.

'Great, I'll look forward to meeting you.'

Anne set up a meeting for a few days' time. I deliberately kept quiet about it among the rest of the team. For a start I had nothing to tell them and I also knew that their minds would go into over-drive if they knew one of Tony Blair's right-hand men was coming into the school. I really couldn't imagine what it was he wanted.

When he arrived on the day, I was immediately surprised. He was much younger than I had expected. He was, however, as smartly dressed as I had imagined and extremely bright and perceptive. He was very charismatic too and had a confidence that is gained from the best the public school educational system can offer.

I didn't push on the agenda for the meeting. Instead I gave Peter a tour of the school and pointed out some of its more wearisome features, such as the unwieldy seven-storey building, which I took him out into the yard to view in its full glory.

Finally, when I had shown him everything, I took him back to my office. Sitting down with a mug of tea, I asked him the question that had been playing on my mind since he'd first made the call.

'So, Peter, what is your interest in Islington Green?'

Peter sat forward in his chair, looking earnest, and took a deep breath. This was something that was clearly important to him. That was obvious by his body language.

'This might seem a little odd,' he began, a little hesitantly. 'I am leaving Number Ten and I would like to come and work on the front line in a school. I'd like to train as a teacher. I believe I have a number of skills that might prove invaluable to Islington Green.'

I did my best to retain a poker face. I hadn't expected this at all.

Perter said he had spoken to Tim Brighouse, the then London schools commissioner: 'I asked Tim the best place to go and he suggested Islington Green. He was very positive about the things you are doing here. He said I should come and talk to you.'

He paused and looked at me for a reaction.

'Oh, well, that is unexpected,' I said, unable to contain my surprise. 'I thought you were here because Islington Green is the school that your boss wouldn't send his son too.'

I scrutinised his face for a reaction. I could see straight away he had completely failed to realise Islington Green's significance in the Downing Street tale.

'Oh God,' he said, as the story sunk in. 'I had completely forgotten about that. Stupidly, I didn't put two and two together.'

He quickly recovered, though.

'That wasn't a good start, was it?' he joked. 'I'm the sort of guy you'd expect to do his research.'

'It was a while back,' I reassured him. 'Plenty has happened since then and a lot of it has been good, believe it or not.

'Listen, on principle I am not against the idea of you coming here. In fact, what is not to like when someone with your communications talents offers his services...'

'I am willing to work unpaid until I am trained,' he interrupted.

'Even better,' I laughed. 'We do, however, have to be mindful of the rest of the team. I know, without a shadow of a doubt, there will be opposition to your coming here. People will inevitably view you as some sort of plant from Number Ten, here to spy on them and make life even more difficult than it already is. We'll have to think very carefully about how to present this.'

Once I was satisfied it wasn't some sort of strange publicity stunt to see off any lingering criticism over Blair's original snub to the school, I welcomed the opportunity to bring Peter into the team. He had a reputation as a sharp intellectual thinker and that was exactly the type of person I needed at my side during the transformation of Islington Green. Although I was aware there would be opposition from those already there, it was a risk worth taking.

After Peter left, I talked it through with Angela and she was encouraging.

'Will he take a turn on the rota for the exclusion room?' she said.

'Yes,' I nodded.

'And the playground duties?'

'Everything,' I confirmed. 'He wants experience on the front line.'

'Then he is in,' she laughed.

'We need to find a teacher he can shadow, someone who won't give him too hard a time,' I said.

'How about Jane Fielding? She's always very flexible and positive and my guess is she would like a posh boy to boss about. Why don't we ask her?'

I smiled. I still hadn't forgotten Jane's first day back at the school, when she had abruptly confronted me in the staff room to ask who I was. I hoped Peter was ready for her.

Something I was reluctant to share with Angela, or indeed anyone else, was one other piece of information Peter had imparted. He wanted to write a book about his experiences in his journey to becoming a teacher. Everyone at Islington Green would have been pretty mistrustful as it was and this sort of news would have ensured out and out hostility towards our new teaching assistant.

I had had two earlier experiences that told me this sort of scrutiny would not go down well. The first occurred shortly after I arrived, when Chris Woodhead, the former Chief Inspector of Schools, got in touch. He had left Ofsted and was now writing for the *Daily Mail,* and he wanted to write a piece about Islington Green. It was later revealed that he had been the person who had ultimately signed the school off into special measures, but at that time the full story wasn't clear, so I gave the profile serious consideration. However, I sounded out Hugh Ritchie, who recommended I spoke to the governors, and they immediately said 'no way'. Their view was the *Daily Mail* would eat us for breakfast and they were probably right. I told Chris thanks but no thanks.

On the second occasion, Channel 4 wanted to film a documentary about the turnaround of the school. I agreed in principle and this time the governors and the local authority were supportive too. However, they did stipulate that I had to get the teachers' agreement, which

I would have had to anyhow, because they would all have to sign disclaimers if they were to appear. This time it was Ken Muller's turn to be vehemently opposed to the idea and he immediately whipped up a storm among the rest of the team, who had initially been non-committal. In a short space of time he managed to get fifty-five teachers to opt out, which made it impossible to continue. I couldn't force them to appear, so that was that.

When it came to Peter's book, I personally didn't object. In fact, I believed it would be very interesting to document the turnaround, However, the only way it was going to happen was if Peter and I kept it to ourselves.

'Won't that make it difficult later on?' Peter asked, when we discussed it.

'It will, but at least the book will be written,' I said. 'My view is we will tell everyone shortly before it is published, although I would like to run it past the leadership team a little earlier than that. Let them read the first draft and if it is going to be a disaster they'll let us know pretty quickly.'

The final hurdle was to get the go ahead from the governors for Peter to join us. When I told them about it, they were very sceptical and most of them were convinced there was some sort of ulterior motive involved.

'I think you should meet him,' I said. 'He comes across very well and I think he could be a real asset.'

Reluctantly they agreed and Peter was summoned to nothing short of an interrogation from the governors. They really grilled him on the real purpose of his career change. He must have convinced them, though, because they gave him a green light.

Peter joined the school in January 2004 as a member of the senior management team. If I thought I'd a baptism by fire at Islington it was probably nothing compared to Peter's. At least I had worked in difficult schools before so had some idea of what to expect. The atmosphere and routine at the school were a far cry from Westminster. Peter had already been at the school for a few days, had had an illuminating guided tour of the school from one of the children, had spent a brief stint manning the exclusion room and had spent time with the SLT when we finally caught up with each other for what was to become a regular Monday afternoon management meeting. I asked him what he thought.

'It's different,' he said, smiling. 'It's difficult not to contrast it with Westminster. The accents have certainly all changed. I've been used to middle class or posh from civil servants, business people and professionals. Here everyone speaks with strong streetwise North London accents.

'It's also interesting to see life outside the Westminster bubble. This is the real world, where people don't buy a newspaper every day and read every line of the news and comment sections. School life doesn't hang on the verdict of the media each morning.'

Old habits must have died hard with Peter, though, because he still resolutely pored over the press each day. Indeed, the office I had allotted him was already piled floor to ceiling with newsprint. When I mentioned it, he smiled.

'Yes, I suppose it is quite hard to change my ways,' he said ruefully. 'I find they help me formulate my ideas. In fact, I was going to ask: when I was at Number Ten, if I had any ideas I would scribble them down and leave them on Tony's desk. If he didn't like them he would just throw them in the bin, but if he did we'd talk about them. Are you comfortable if I do that with you?'

'Yes,' I agreed, wondering what sort of ideas he might come up with. 'If it's good enough for the Prime Minister then it's good enough for me.'

I couldn't help but be curious about what Peter would bring to the party from the political world and asked him straight out what it was he most thought we should change.

He thought for a few moments before giving his response.

'One of the biggest things that has struck me going around the school is just how many new initiatives you are juggling at the same time. Each one has a big implication for the future of the school and has a good reason for happening but I am worried they are not having the impact they should.

'It is hard for the staff to make sense of what is important with so much going on.'

He had a point. Just thinking through the staff bulletins I regularly sent out, there seemed to be something new to say nearly every day. There were new school rules, ideas on the exclusion room, initiatives to deal with the prevalence of mobile phones, instructions on new merit schemes. The list was endless.

'It seems to me that more thought needs to go into the delivery of the message,' Peter went on. 'You may benefit from boiling it all down into a few key headline-grabbing objectives and then let everything else flow from there. It's a technique that has served political leaders well and could even be said to be the bedrock of New Labour's success.'

He had a point. It would certainly help in making staff feel less overwhelmed.

'What is it you want the school to be?' he asked.

I thought about that for a short while. Right then I had a very long list.

'I want it to calm down,' I said at last. 'I want the teachers to stop fussing and treating every day like we're in the middle of a crisis. I want the parents to stop panicking about what is being done and above all I want the children to calm down and behave properly.'

The key to the smooth running of any school is to ensure children are in the right place at the right time and in the right mood to absorb what they are being told. To turn around any difficult school, the first step is to get the behaviour right. In my view, the order of priority should always be behaviour, attendance and then achievement. If a school is calm and children turn up every day, better results will automatically follow. A calm school won't just benefit the children either. It is the key to everything else that goes on in the school.

The idea of a calm school was born and Peter added to it by suggesting I present the message as though everyone was on a journey together towards our calm, productive future. From then on, everything was to be tied into the psychology of calmness and I wasted no opportunity in getting the vision across.

Chapter seven

CONTINUOUS DEVELOPMENT

⸻

During my twenty-seven years of working as a teacher in schools, I was observed just three times: once by my PGCE tutor, then by an Ofsted inspector and then by my head of department. Other than that, over nearly three decades, I didn't receive any coaching either formally or informally, or indeed any feedback on my teaching whatsoever or on how to improve what I was doing. Faced with this vacuum I did the best I could and did what I still see pretty much every teacher do: I followed the lead of a teacher I admired. In my case it was my economics teacher Stanley Rolls, who taught me from 1974 to 1978 at Sunbury Grammar School in Surrey. I was fortunate that he also shared with me an invaluable piece of advice, which was: 'Don't talk throughout the whole lesson; you'll just irritate the children.'

'I always think of the sixty-minute lesson as being divided into twenty, twenty, twenty,' he explained. 'That means twenty minutes of talking, even though sometimes that is a bit too much, twenty minutes of questions and answers or doing an exercise, and twenty minutes watching a video and making notes.'

That pretty much describes my teaching style ever since, although, while I relentlessly stick to the principle, experience has shown me the proportions are a little out. It should really be nearer ten, thirty, ten and definitely no more than twenty minutes of talking. I've been in classes where teachers talked for forty minutes or more and wondered why the children were starting to get restless. They don't seem to understand they've lost them after a few minutes (boys sooner than girls!) unless they're very engaging indeed.

Even if schools do understand the need for some sort of training programme, the implementation is usually so informal as to be next to useless. It will be left to someone on the SLT to take charge of learning and coaching. Then, because they work in the school and perhaps have to meet a difficult parent who may be coming in that day, a planned training session will be moved, or quietly dropped altogether. Time after time there will be all sorts of reasons why it doesn't happen and, before anyone knows it, twenty-seven years will fly by without any formal assessment. Even if there is a coaching session, most people are reluctant to take advice from a close colleague, however well intended.

There is a clear case for a formal training scheme, preferably with experienced help coming from outside the school so there is no possibility of anyone becoming distracted.

One of the most effective educational initiatives that the Blair government introduced was the London Challenge. At the time it first appeared, in 2003, parents were fleeing inner London to avoid sending their children to local schools, yet today pupils from the capital are more likely to perform well than those anywhere else in the country. The policy centred around school collaboration and a core group of London Challenge advisers who gave support to underperforming schools in a handful of key boroughs. They were given a budget of around £1 million a year per school, on top of each school's main budget, to, among other things, work to improve professional standards among teachers. This mentoring-based model included help for the heads of each school.

Something that came as a shock to me early in my career was coming across teachers who were not clear on what children should be learning in individual lessons. In schools that are failing it is common for teachers to have little understanding of learning objectives, and my Queen's tour of Islington Green uncovered a number of instances of this. Teachers would confidently begin a lesson declaring something like, 'Today we are going to do exercise three on page twenty-eight.' They'd set tasks without being clear in their own minds what it was the children needed to learn that day.

Continuous development

One of my most memorable examples of this came when I sat in on a Year 11 art class very early on. It was a fairly low ability class and when I arrived the children were diligently colouring some shapes from a Rothko painting in what I assumed to be a project to do with reductionist art. It had all the hallmarks of a rather unchallenging Blue Peter or Mister Maker session.

I turned to a couple of girls and said, 'This is lovely. What are you doing today?'

'We're making a shiny, sparkly version of a Rothko painting,' said one of the girls, who told me her name was Louise.

'Do you know what sort of art Rothko does?' I asked.

'No.'

I turned to Louise's friend, a fellow Year 11 who was called Sarah. She was concentrating hard on painting on one side of a piece of paper and then rubbing it down onto another.

'That's an interesting technique,' I said, encouragingly. 'Did you learn this today?'

'No, we used to do this in Year 7,' she said with a shrug, standing back to admire her work.

On face value, it was a great art class. The kids were well behaved and there were some beautiful things on the wall. However, I had to tell the art teacher, Josie, that if it had been a session with an Ofsted inspector it would have been classed as inadequate.

'What were you trying to get them to learn today?' I asked.

Josie looked a bit taken aback and said, 'It was a study of reductionist art.'

'Except the word "reductionist" wasn't mentioned?'

'Well, yes, that is a bit too complicated for this class,' she said, her voice trailing off.

When pressed, Josie was able to confidently explain the theory behind a Rothko painting and how the artist takes landscapes and reduces them to particular colours you might see on the horizon. Yet the children didn't know that. They would have learned something if she had told them that.

Teachers need to be really clear about what they want their charges to learn. If they are going to study reductionist art, tell them they are studying reductionist art. If they are learning how to multiply, be clear on that learning objective. Showing teachers how to create credible learning objectives and other similar techniques transforms their performance in a very short space of time.

Ensuring my staff set letting learning objectives was just one small part of the programme of continuous improvement I kicked off at Islington Green. Another was to encourage them all to give more thought to the psychology of learning. Many teachers, unless, of course, they studied psychology at university, have never given it much thought. Yet it can have a huge impact.

Most people understand that a person's upbringing can have a substantial effect on the way they see the world. If a child's parents are oppressive, it is quite likely this will translate into rebellious behaviour in the classroom.

Continuous development

A child with controlling parents who do everything for them is never going to be much of an independent thinker. Then there are the children with anxious helicopter parents. They are ferried from one activity to another: first it is football, then they spend time at a youth club before being whisked off to a theatre school, and so on. There are the kids who are always hyperactive, simply because they can't get to grips with the notion of settling down in one place. Each of these children will have different needs in the classroom and will present differing challenges.

I was discussing this issue with Angela and Emma when I was reminded of Bloom's taxonomy, the foundation of the modern national curriculum. Benjamin Bloom was one of the first people to recognise that everyone has a different way of thinking and we don't all think with the same level of sophistication. While Bloom's six categories of learning (knowledge, comprehension, application, analysis, synthesis and evaluation) are well known, it is quite rare to see them properly understood or applied in the classroom. Yet, following on from my above point on learning objectives, it makes sense to set those objectives at the right level for each child, even though there will be a range of abilities and levels in any class. This may mean three or four learning objectives per lesson to target each ability group, so different levels can access what they need. This is key to getting overall results up. It will bring on every group regardless of ability, which is far more effective than simply teaching to the middle in the blind hope every child will derive at least some benefit. All that does is hold back the bright kids and alienate the ones who can't keep up, and it is not much good for the ones it is targeted at either.

Teachers are, as I discovered at Islington Green, often reluctant to run their lessons on this basis. I was, however, keen to demonstrate how effective 'chunking' could be.

'I will take any lesson and demonstrate the practicalities to you,' I told the assembled and somewhat cynical team after dropping the bombshell that I wanted them to change the way they taught.

The class chosen for the demonstration was being taught by the head of geography, Geraldine Smith, and to kick off I asked Geraldine to explain what she was planning to do in the lesson.

'We're learning about volcanoes,' she said, clearly less than happy to be chosen as the guinea pig. 'To begin with I will give them the page we need to turn to, to find the volcano chapter of the reference book. Then we will discuss the seven characteristics of a volcano outlined there. The children will make notes and then draw and label a volcano.'

It was all interesting as far as it went, but it didn't really further individual knowledge. My view was the lesson should be tacked completely differently.

The Year 10 children looked slightly bemused to see me taking the class and as a result were unusually quiet. To start off, I asked them to open their textbooks and find the volcanoes chapter. They didn't need to be told what page to turn to because they were perfectly intelligent and could use a table of contents. Besides, if we stop spoon feeding them by giving them page numbers, it helps them start to learn by themselves.

Once they had found the chapter, I told them to turn the book over and not look at it.

'Now,' I said. 'Turn to the person next to you and, working together, write fourteen things you already know about volcanoes on the piece of paper in front of you. You can draw a volcano if you like, but I don't want you to spend too long on it.'

The children looked quite energised as they spoke in pairs about a subject they clearly already knew quite a lot about. When I collected all the papers together we had more than 100 facts about volcanoes. The kids had written about where they were, which countries had the most, places that people had died in the lava following an eruption, the whole nine yards.

I then allocated six facts to each child and asked them to look in the book to find out as much as they could about those six things. They were to make short notes to present to their friend. Unbeknown to the children, I geared the activities to their ability range. The less able kids were asked to look up some basic facts in their standard textbooks for their presentation. Meanwhile, the brighter kids were asked to direct their research further afield.

'Volcanoes are dangerous, so find me some methods for predicting volcanic activity and therefore making them less threatening to humans,' I told them.

Every child in the room was given an activity according to their ability even though the tasks sounded the same to them. By chunking the work, I was able to appeal to some children's evaluative and creative skills while at the same time inspiring other children by getting them to record simple facts. If I hadn't done this, some children who already understood the topic would very quickly have got bored. Equally, if the less able children hadn't been able to access the level of learning relevant to them, they would most likely have become discouraged and would probably have become disruptive too.

By the end of the lesson the children seemed genuinely happy and inspired but Geraldine was even less impressed than when we began. She didn't say it, but she was obviously thinking, 'Oh, very clever – now my next lesson is going to seem *really* interesting, isn't it?'

Geraldine had a point too. All I had proved with this exercise was what a clever dick I was. I hadn't really helped the teacher at all. I had just made her life more difficult. What I should have done, and indeed did start to do, was to arrange coaching for her so she too could understand how to set learning objectives and chunk her classes. It can take a term to do this, but it is far more effective than the way Geraldine had previously been teaching her classes.

When teachers set learning objectives, they need to look at children's past achievements to put them into the right ability levels. There can be three or four ability groups in a single class and lessons need to be based around those levels of learning. Once teachers know these levels, they can set tiered learning objectives to reinforce the things pupils need to know during a lesson. All the children could do a particular task, or just some of them could do it, with the rest doing something more appropriate to their ability. Kids need some easy wins and these can be achieved in a variety of ways, but reinforcing that basic learning ability is key.

The big problem at Islington Green was that the previous attempts at training had been too haphazard. There were more than half a dozen organisations from outside the school that purported to be offering coaching services, from City Challenge to Education Action Zone to the local authority, but it was all a bit directionless. Every organisation had a different agenda, so, although it looked like there was a lot of activity going on, this didn't translate into any sort of unified strategic vision.

There was a clear need for a formalised programme of regular training sessions at Islington Green. We couldn't just leave training to the odd burst of activity once a year on inset days. I began with a 'learning review', which meant that each month we focussed on one of the ten faculties, such as languages, science or maths. Outside advisers would be brought in to review the teaching and identify weaknesses and then asked to develop an action plan. The review and training elements were then presented to the governing body so they could act as a sounding board and evaluate what we were doing. After each department was reviewed we developed a whole-school action plan that focussed on coaching in the classroom for teachers, mid-level leaders and the most senior members of the team. Experienced heads and deputies from other schools were invited in to work with our team to develop the skills of the Islington Green teachers. After-school training sessions were organised every three weeks and each one tackled a new element. There were sessions on setting learning objectives, ones on planning and others on assessment techniques. Training became a constant process that we didn't allow to lapse.

Another initiative we took advantage of were a number of London Challenge training courses for deputies and heads. One was a thirty-day training course called Leading for Success. London Challenge offered to pay the full £12,000 fee to train the whole SLT team in a series of residential sessions that focussed on skills such as team building, strategic planning and listening and coaching. I couldn't see what we had to lose by signing up for it. There were some in the SLT, most notably Paul Blum, who thought it was all a bit of wishy-washy nonsense. Paul was so disillusioned he wrote to the *TES* to say so. Although some of it was nonsense, we were shown some useful techniques too. One of the most useful of these, which they called Brown Paper Planning, turned out to be spot on for Islington Green. Brown Paper Planning was all about how to structure a meeting to get a positive outcome. Anything that would help keep meetings on track sounded like a good idea to me.

To be fair, I had made some headway with meetings.

Before I joined, meetings at Islington Green had been legendary. Marion would begin them at 5pm and they'd go on until 9, at which point the wine would come out. I was determined meetings would be an hour and a half maximum because, in my view, if you can't get it all done in an hour, you shouldn't bother. It was always a bit of a struggle to stick to this aim, though. The problem we had was, well, everyone always had a problem with any idea put forward. If I went into a meeting and said, 'We have an issue with behaviour and what we need to do is this and this,' there would always be someone who popped up to say, 'I can see that is a good idea, but the problem with that solution is….' Or, someone would be eager to share their experience of when they had tried something before and it didn't quite work out.

In Brown Paper Planning the process is *all* about coming up with ideas. The person leading the meeting makes sure everyone knows that no one is allowed to say anything to shoot the ideas down. The moment anyone starts up, the meeting leader says, 'Remember the rules: no negative comments. Everyone will get the chance to evaluate all the ideas at the end of the meeting. That is when we will decide whether there are any killer problems and if there are solutions to the killer problems.' The Brown Paper part is that you literally write up the ideas on brown paper parcel, which you stick onto the wall, in the style of the *CSI* TV programme when they evaluate all the evidence.

It really works, too. It stops people being negative and gets them talking. Invariably, you end up with an idea that can work and it is easier to find a way around any problems. The meeting is succinct and at the end you have a plan of action. What is not to like?

London Challenge also contributed greatly by allocating mentors to deputies and heads. Guidance and support from an expert in the field will help anyone advance much quicker than if they are left to do things on their own, and I was keen to introduce it at Islington Green.

Of course, this strategy stands or falls on the quality of the mentor. In my first headship I was allocated a supposedly experienced mentor and could tell from the very first session it was never going to work. He spent the first half an hour of our hour-long session moaning about his school and how he was struggling to control many of the children. The remainder of the session was no more inspiring. I ended that arrangement very rapidly and turned to my own ex-head, Hugh Richie, whom I did respect. I paid him to spend an afternoon with me and then we made an arrangement where he was on the end of the phone if I ever needed advice. Another useful resource early in my career as a head teacher was the helpline of the Association of Secondary Headteachers in Essex and I am not afraid to admit that I was on the phone to them a lot in the early days at Mayfield School.

There are a lot of things they just don't tell you on the (non-existent) training course on how to be a headmaster or deputy. One of my first challenges at Islington Green, for example, was how to deal with a music teacher who had run up a bill of £500 on his classroom telephone *while* he was supposedly teaching classes. It was obviously wrong and he shouldn't have been doing it, but I didn't know exactly how to deal with the situation. I had a chat with Hugh Richie and he advised that firstly I should find out who it was he kept calling, secondly I should present him with an invoice for £500 and thirdly I should set out the disciplinary policy.

It turned out the calls were all to the teacher's mistress. The woman was rather bemused to receive a call from a headmaster but helpfully told me all I needed to know. I presented the chap with a bill and began the disciplinary procedure. He was a bit of a slippery character, though, and clearly decided the best way to keep his phone bill down would be to skip out of school to see his lover. That didn't end well for the music teacher.

The problems that confront a head teacher change all the time, but having another, experienced head as a sounding board makes a huge difference. By the same token, I have a lot of experience that I am willing to share with my deputies. I repeatedly said to the senior team at Islington Green, 'Call me any time if you have problems. It doesn't matter how stupid it might seem.'

At first, people were reluctant and said they didn't want to waste my time.

I always said, 'You are not wasting my time. My business is making this school succeed. If a stupid decision is made, then we don't succeed. If it's a good decision then we do succeed.' Eventually senior colleagues learn what your view is likely to be.

This doesn't mean I needed to wade in and sort out every problem personally. Sometimes just a few words are enough. In my first few weeks, for example, there was a huge panic among the senior team over a relationship between two of the younger teachers. The man and woman had been dating and it had ended rather badly. So badly, in fact, they couldn't bear being in the same room as one another. When they did come across each other around the school they would loudly trade insults.

'What do you want to do about it?' demanded Hannah at the SLT meeting. 'He is being really aggressive to her. God knows where this is going to end.'

'I think you're probably going to have to step in and talk to them,' agreed Paul.

There was a murmur of agreement among the others. This had clearly been the main topic of conversation for a few days.

'I agree this is very serious, but I am not going to talk to them,' I said. 'Angela, I want you to go back and say to them both that this is a private matter. They have had a relationship and have fallen out. However, if they have another argument in school this will be taken as misconduct because they won't be doing their jobs. Let them know that I have said they will be disciplined. They should keep it outside school and deal with it themselves.'

Although the matter had occupied an inordinate amount of the SLT's emotional energy, as far as I was concerned, this was nothing to do with us *unless* it was affecting the school. Letting it become a big thing was a distraction. We needed to deal with it and move on. That is exactly what we did. There is a temptation to get involved with staff on an emotional rather than a professional level. Like toddlers they will keep behaving this way for attention. Attention should be reserved for professional performance.

Any teacher in a senior position would benefit from a good mentor who is committed to helping them learn what is needed to become better at their job. A mentor is not just there to assist with learning essential skills and knowledge but also to provide a deeper understanding of how a school functions and how best to work with the different personalities it contains.

One issue I have always been acutely aware of, especially working in inner-city schools, is that teachers are often afraid of their students. They are not just afraid of some sort of physical assault, which can happen, but are worried about getting things wrong. There are such high expectations placed on schools and teachers today that sometimes it is hard to know which way to turn. Parents want this, governors want that, the local authority something else, the secretary of state more, Ofsted is checking this and the head teacher is checking that. With so many masters watching, there is bound to be tension created.

It is for this reason that, while I was entirely focussed on training and continuous improvement at Islington

Green, I also realised that it couldn't just all be about work. If all I did was bang on about development, training and doing this, that and the other to improve results, I would very quickly have a demoralised team. Teams, like schools, can get into incredibly negative cycles. When everything seems like one battle after another and teachers are constantly being asked to step up to the plate, they begin to feel exhausted, let down and unappreciated. Not surprisingly, it sometimes becomes hard to see the positive side of things at all. It is for this reason that I turned my mind to finding ways to introduce an element of fun and enjoyment for both staff and children.

Earlier in my career at Alec Hunter, I was put in charge of a curriculum initiative called TVEI, which was an intervention to encourage the use of technology and vocational education. It did neither brilliantly well, but it poured a lot of money into schools when it was needed. I was given a budget of £40,000 to spend on it, spread across a couple of years. My predecessors in this endeavour had spent the budget on various worthy activities such as buying computers for classes, books for the library or training for staff. To be honest, though, each successive attempt had made a negligible difference. It seemed pretty obvious we needed to try something different.

Pondering the various options, I reflected on events I had been to with my then wife, Jennifer. She worked in the City and, it being the eighties boom time for financial institutions, barely a week went by without one flashy bash or another. Banks would take over venues such as the British Museum, a Thames riverboat or a large stately home and the champagne would flow. I even got to tag along as Jennifer's plus one on a corporate jolly to Venice. Although the speeches that invariably accompanied these events were tedious, there were always lots of interesting people to talk to and it was easy to see how unifying the events were for those who worked in the various financial institutions. I often thought that when I got into a position of any influence I would try to do something along these lines. Now, here was my opportunity.

At Alec Hunter, I suggested to Hugh Richie that we organised something I called Curricular Island Days (CIDs) once every half term throughout the year. We would spend £6,000 on each one and set up numerous events in the lead up to the day itself. Hugh, who was always tremendously supportive, told me to go ahead and try it.

I decided the days would all be themed and had to have an educational focus, but most importantly they had to be fun. To kick it off, the first one centred around personal social education, because that gave me a broad sweep to work with. I set about organising a series of activities that would inevitably get everyone to sit up and take notice. I invited a theatre company into the school to do a play focussed on the theme. At lunchtime, I brought in magicians to go around the tables performing magic tricks for the kids and staff. In the evening, there was a dedicated event for staff with entertainment from a band and a motivational speaker.

The day after the first event, staff kept stopping me in the corridors to say, 'Wow, what happened yesterday? This has never happened in our school before.'

They were genuinely enthusiastic and motivated. Better still, they were uplifted by the prospect of another event only a matter of weeks away. They couldn't wait to find out what I had up my sleeve and had plenty of suggestions of their own.

It didn't take much time before staff began to build rewards schemes into their teaching schedules, all geared towards the CIDs. If the kids got behaviour merits in every lesson, on the day itself their teacher would take them to the park for a field trip based on the theme. Others organised sponsored activities around the days.

As the idea of the CIDs took off, I became more ambitious. I remembered a head from my first school who had, for some unknown reason, got a helicopter to land in the school field to pick him up. It then dropped him in the middle of nowhere and he had to find his way back. At the time we all thought it was rather perverse. However, I did recall that the kids found the idea of a helicopter landing on a field amazing. There was educational value in seeing a helicopter and chatting to the pilot too. So, I hired a helicopter for one of the CIDs. The kids who behaved best in the run up to the day got a short ride in the helicopter, as did the head, Hugh. They were taken to a nearby airfield and sponsored to make their own way back. It cost just £600 to hire the helicopter, but the value to the children and staff was enormous. Everyone was talking about it and brimming with different ideas about what we could do with the helicopter next time.

The activities built up to end-of-term functions solely for the staff. In the summer, for example, we'd have an outdoor event where everyone would sit around drinking lukewarm beer and watching a band. While working at the school was often challenging, we made it a fun place to be too.

The naysayers would probably say, 'What the hell is that all about? Budgets are stretched enough as it is – wouldn't you be better off spending the money elsewhere?'

Whenever anyone said this to me, and they frequently did, my reply would always be the same: 'We are spending money on the most important assets in the place, which are teachers and the children. If the teachers are positive about the place, they are positive with the children, and if the children are positive the results are positive. That is how it works.'

In a transformational situation, there is no point waiting until things are better before you start enjoying the process. Fun is part of the way to make it work. If you opt to wait until it is working before you relax and enjoy it, you will never get there.

Even though teaching is a profession like no other, few people turn up at work every day for the sheer joy of it. They want to be rewarded, and not just financially either. Individuals are obviously motivated by different things, but that doesn't mean motivation should be left to chance. It is possible to take a systematic approach to recognising and rewarding the team for their sterling efforts in helping to transform a school.

One of the most powerful motivational tools at our disposal are the little acts that say 'we know what you do' and 'thank you'. If you want loyalty out of your people, you have to demonstrate it in return. This means putting in place measures to show you care about them and the conditions they work in. It also means you have to think about having fun now and again.

Injecting a bit of fun and levity can be done in the smallest of ways. For example, I always tried to start staff meetings with a joke or a funny story. Sometimes I would say, 'OK, this is what you are going to do anyway, so let's get this out of the way. Turn to the person next to you and talk to them about your holidays. You have three minutes.'

At Islington Green, I put in place regular events such as 'No such thing as a free lunch day' where we gave out free pizzas in the staff room on the last Friday of the month. At the end of term I would take the whole team out for a meal at a local restaurant. (There were still the odd conscientious objectors who refused to go because they thought it was an inappropriate use of school funds.) On training days I would break things up a bit by bringing in a comedian or some jugglers or by arranging for everyone to have a massage if they wanted one.

I pooled the kitty for training staff, which had previously gone on all sorts of random jollies, and gave the money to the heads of each faculty. I said, 'Here is a £1,000 budget for the year. You can use it to take your staff for a meal, go off to do some training, or to take everyone to a hotel for a weekend to do a bit of educational bonding.'

I just wanted to encourage the team to be a bit more human with each other and feel special about themselves and where they worked.

In the spring of 2004, I had the idea of holding our annual end-of-year awards event at Sadler's Wells theatre. This was when we awarded GCSE certificates, and prizes to the best students in other years. I saw it as a great opportunity to not only demonstrate the school was on the way up after a hairy few years but also incentivise good behaviour – that is, demonstrate the positive part of positive discipline. Children were told about the event and that a limited number of seats would be available at this prestigious venue. Only children who had purple badges for attendance on their blazers, or a gold certificate for 100 merits, would be on the guest list. To add a further incentive, I entrusted Peter Hyman with the task of bringing in a 'celebrity' guest speaker. Ideally, I wanted his old boss, Tony Blair, but Peter said it was unlikely he'd attend, particularly in the light of the fact of the previous criticism he'd earned for not sending his son to the school. However, Peter did think he might get Tony's legendary sharp-tongued communications chief, Alastair Campbell.

When I outlined my idea in the staff room, many of the staff were openly sceptical, including some members of the SLT.

'That's not going to work,' said Paul. 'All the geeks who have been hiding away in fear of being beaten up aren't suddenly going to begin parading around showing off purple badges on their lapels.'

'I don't agree,' I said. 'I think if we make it exciting enough everyone will want to come.'

And I was right. Kids were soon lining up asking how they could get a place. Peter was true to his word and, as well as securing Alastair, also got in Joe Swash, who played Mickey Miller in *EastEnders*, to hand out some of the performing-arts prizes. (It is worth noting that not all the members of staff were as impressed and a couple boycotted the event because of Campbell's presence.)

We had roughly 400 children at the first Sadler's Wells event, which, although it was a noisy, rowdy affair, was an evening to remember. When I returned to the school in September I was stopped at least forty times in the corridor by children asking about it.

'What's this Sadler's Wells business then, sir?'

'Why didn't I get invited?'

'I heard that Sol Campbell came.' (He didn't, but there was no harm giving the impression he may very well come next time.)

I explained to everyone who was interested that to earn a place they needed a purple badge or to have earned enough merits. This didn't put them off and the following year 600 children had done enough to be invited along. The event expanded each year I was there and truth be told it got a bit out of hand, but I was on a roll by then.

Chapter eight

POLITICAL AND MEDIA SCRUTINY

One aspect of my Islington Green journey that I hadn't fully anticipated was how deeply it would draw me into the world of politics. Although the shadow of Tony Blair was never far away from us, I was a little surprised by the level of scrutiny from Westminster. In addition to Peter Hyman's sharp political insight, I was also subjected to the benefit of observations from no fewer than seven visiting lords (including Lord Puttnam, Lord Adonis and Lord Hattersley), several government ministers and (at the Sadler's Wells event) Blair's ubiquitous spokesperson, Alastair Campbell. We were also, at one stage, host to the entire Japanese cabinet, and received near-weekly visits from heads of one educational/leadership/youth (delete as appropriate) group or another.

Most of the visits went pretty smoothly, bar one. I was

just about to have a meeting with Lord Adonis, the then Minister of State for Education, when I was interrupted by a phone call from a somewhat breathless English teacher.

'I need to see you outside now,' he said.

'I really can't come now. I'm about to meet with the minister,' I said, wondering what could possibly be so urgent.

'There is a problem in the playground,' he said, his voice sounding more urgent now.

'What is the problem?'

I heard a pause and a deep breath from the other end.

'There's a bit of a riot going on. Our resident community police offer has cuffed a child and restrained her by sitting on her. It's turned quite ugly out here.'

'I'll be straight out.'

We, like all schools, had recently been assigned our own police officer. It was a populist Blair idea that I had my doubts about, but on balance I considered that any support in the playground would be quite helpful. How wrong I turned out to be. It had all kicked off when a teacher had shouted 'stop that girl' because one of the Year 10s was about to walk off the premises. Inexplicably, 'our' policewoman leaped up, jumped on the pupil and wrestled her to the ground *Sweeney*-style, finishing the take-down by putting her captive's arms behind her back and cuffing her. As if that wasn't bad enough, she ended her routine by sitting on the girl to prevent her trying to escape. The other kids went ballistic. It took quite a lot of sorting out, but it was a very real demonstration to the minister that these well-meaning initiatives do sometimes need more thought.

In between all these visits from politicians and while trying to carry out all the reforms they were so keen to understand, I was invited to Number Ten in May 2004, where I met Blair himself. The cool thing to say here would be that I took it all in my stride, but if I am honest it was a bit of a head turner for a young lad from Surrey.

Peter had set up the visit to Downing Street because he was keen for me to become more involved in politics.

'I don't know – just because I can yarn on for a while, you lot think I would make a great MP,' I joked with him.

He laughed but assured me that finding a place for me in the New Labour vision was a deadly serious proposition. The first step was to meet Blair's then fixer, Sally Morgan, and so off we went.

We'd only just got through the security checks when Gordon Brown ambled past, carrying a big bundle of papers.

'Hello, Peter,' he said smiling but at the same time looking a little confused. 'I thought you had left. What are you doing back here?'

Peter explained what he was doing back in Number Ten and introduced me to Gordon, who was very encouraging. Minutes later I was speaking to Alistair Darling, who had also stopped to say hello to Peter. Then, Blair himself turned up.

'Peter,' he boomed. 'You're back.'

'Just for a short while, Tony,' he said, shaking the Prime Minister's hand warmly. 'I'd like you to meet Trevor Averre-Beeson, the head of Islington Green. He is here to see Sally.'

'Trevor,' he said, gripping my hand firmly and shaking it. 'It's great to finally meet you. How are you getting on in Islington?'

I did my best to give a rapid, yet positive, appraisal of the school and what we were doing to address its problems. Even though this was an unscheduled chat, I was surprised at how well informed Blair was. His questions demonstrated an intense knowledge and understanding of the issues. He was also supremely pleasant and, well, normal. He had his people skills down to a tee.

We talked for about five or ten minutes, but it was obvious the Prime Minister's aide was getting quite agitated about the time. He was practically hopping from foot to foot as he very pointedly looked at his watch. Blair was clearly needed elsewhere. It was not long since the *Daily Mirror* had published photos that appeared to show the torture of an Iraqi prisoner by British soldiers and the Prime Minister was about to hold urgent talks with his advisers. (The photos were later revealed to be a hoax and the *Daily Mirror's* editor, Piers Morgan, was sacked.)

'How is it playing out there?' he asked as he excused himself to go to the meeting. 'What are the people saying about it?'

I wasn't quite sure if I understood him properly.

'What do you mean, on the TV?' I asked.

'No, no, in the workplace. In your home.'

'People are not saying much at all,' I answered truthfully, because as far as I was aware there had not been much discussion in the corridors and playgrounds of Islington. 'It is mainly *Guardian* readers and politicians who are most concerned.'

Blair nodded thoughtfully and went on his way.

My political aspirations came to naught in the end, but the episode was an interesting insight into the differences between the two worlds.

Intense political scrutiny was not the only external factor to deal with during my time at Islington Green. I was also firmly on the media radar. Most weeks I'd get a call from a print or broadcast journalist inquiring about my thoughts on this story or that and, because I was always willing to speak fairly candidly, they kept coming back. While I was willing to discuss my general views on dealing with disruptive pupils, falling grades and varying teaching standards, I was always careful in the way I couched my commentary. I had learned the hard way how powerful a force the press can be when they sniff out an interesting angle.

When I was at Alec Hunter and first had success with positive discipline, I had shared my enthusiasm in the school's weekly newsletter. I took the opportunity to record a some details about the thinking behind the approach and the widespread benefits of its success. To illustrate how far we'd come in such a short space of time, I cited some earlier research I had done when I had first become deputy. I'd sent out a questionnaire asking whether pupils had experienced any bullying in the past year and 98 per cent of respondents had said they had. In addition, 94 per cent agreed that they had themselves bullied someone. When I had done the research I had been a little surprised the figure was so high. I'd put it down to the fact it had been quite an unscientific survey and I hadn't been terribly precise in my definition of bullying. When I explored the matter further at the time it emerged that some children defined bullying as a few cruel taunts in the playground. Since we'd introduced positive discipline, the anecdotal evidence was that low-level bullying had all but disappeared and the more serious incidences had become virtually unheard of. This seemed worth noting in the report.

As always, I sent out a copy of the newsletter to the local paper, the *Braintree & Witham Times*. I did that every week and most of the time they ignored it. This time, at best all I hoped for was a few lines deep into the paper saying something like 'behaviour improves at local school thanks to new initiative'.

When the next edition of the *Braintree & Witham Times* landed on my desk, I could hardly believe my eyes. The page-one splash had a banner headline in two-inch black letters that screamed, '98 per cent of children at Alec Hunter High School bullied'. I had barely mentioned the earlier bullying survey in my newsletter and then only to illustrate the range of ways positive discipline had transformed the school, yet the newspaper had turned the story on its head. Reading the copy with a sinking heart, I saw they had noted that things were changing, but this was buried in the copy and clearly the damage had been done.

I went straight to Hugh Richie's office to apologise.

'I really hadn't expected them to do that,' I said, feeling a little foolish for my naivety with the media.

'All publicity is good publicity,' Hugh said cheerily with a wave of his hand. 'It'll blow over in a few days,' he assured me confidently.

It didn't. In fact, it got a lot, lot worse. A local stringer seized the story and sold it on to the one place guaranteed to not just give it a home but ratchet it up a notch or two on the hysterical publicity scale: the *Daily Mail*. After that, it was picked up everywhere. Alec Hunter featured on *BBC News*, on *London Tonight* and in several national broadsheets and magazines.

Although I was helpless to deal with the rate at which the story spread and the angle the reporters took, I did have enough marketing training to know there is no point hiding when something like this happens. If you leave a news vacuum, the media will simply fill in their own details or go off in search of someone who will say what they want. I answered their calls and stepped up to say positive discipline was sorting everything out.

'This is not an issue unique to Alec Hunter,' I told journalists. 'However, we have found a unique way of addressing it and our results have been phenomenal.'

Gradually, over the next few, uncomfortable, days, the furore began to die down. However, the media had one more rude shock in store for me. I received a call from a researcher from the daytime chat show *Kilroy*, hosted by the former MP Robert Kilroy-Silk.

'We're very interested in your work on bullying,' she said. 'We were wondering if you would be able to bring some children onto the show to discuss it. It would be very powerful to get a kid's eye view, as it were.

'Ideally, we would like a mix of children, some who have been bullied and some who have been bullies themselves.'

There was no way I was even going to consider rounding up some self-confessed bullies, but I did agree to bring a group of sixth formers to the show. I was careful to pick a group of intelligent, articulate and presentable kids and did my best to brief them on what to expect. Even so, I was pretty nervous about what might happen.

When we arrived at the studio, Kilroy-Silk was his usual confrontational self and certainly not fazed by the group of nervous seventeen-year-olds who'd been put in front of him. Pushing his microphone into the face of one of the girls, Jayne, he came out with his first question.

'Have you been bullied?'

'Yes,' Jayne said.

'What happened?'

Jayne, who had been prepared for the question, answered in an honest and mature way. As soon as she had finished, Kilroy-Silk nodded thoughtfully.

He said: 'Sometimes people who have been bullied have been bullies too. Did you ever bully?'

Jayne stared at the host. It was clear she had been caught off guard by the question. Then, after a lengthy pause, she broke down.

'Yes, I have,' she said, biting back the tears.

Then, with a bit of prompting by Kilroy-Silk, she haltingly described a time when she and a couple of girlfriends had picked on another girl. For Kilroy-Silk, it was chat-show gold. I was gutted that it had happened and Jayne's parents were understandably pretty unimpressed too. Following the show, I wrote to Kilroy-Silk and said I thought he had been unfair. I wasn't expecting much of a response and sure enough I got a dismissive note from one of his researchers saying, in effect, 'It's the business we're in.'

The experience taught me a lot about dealing with the media, but in the main part at least the intense reaction gave me an opportunity to get across what could be achieved with positive discipline. The publicity following the bullying report enabled me in a very rapid way to get this new attitude to teaching on the map in the UK.

My experience at Alec Hunter was excellent preparation for Islington Green. Since Tony Blair had taken his son Euan elsewhere, the school had constantly been under intense media scrutiny. From the moment I arrived I felt under siege. I got the impression that the press and broadcast media were waiting for one of two things. Either the school would implode, thus vindicating the Prime Minister's decision, or we would deliver the slightly better news version where the school would rise to unimaginable heights of success, thus proving what lousy judgement Blair possessed. While I was not interested in point scoring – indeed, I always privately felt Blair might have had a point taking his son elsewhere at that time – I obviously preferred the latter option.

Most of the time I was happy to talk openly to the media, which meant they kept coming back, asking me to comment on educational stories whether or not they directly affected Islington Green. Teachers TV was in the school all the time and made five or six documentaries with various people from the school. Whenever there was a big education story in the press we were asked to host interviews with politicians talking in the playground and I was frequently brought in to comment at the same time. I long suspected this irked some of the other heads in the area and this was confirmed to me when I was called out of a heads' conference at the London Art House to do an urgent interview for *BBC News*. Lord Adonis had just been named as Education Minister and since he was a local resident the BBC thought it appropriate for me to comment. A few of the other heads made their disapproval known in no uncertain terms.

Islington Green was the backdrop to a number of TV shows on CBBC and CBeebies and was also used as a location for the British psychological thriller *Notes on a Scandal,* staring Judy Dench, Cate Blanchett and Bill Nighy. I didn't mind the media presence too much and the kids loved it. The only time it began to grate was around the anniversary of the release of Pink Floyd's album *The Wall*. We would have up to five film crews from all over the world besieging the school, desperate to film 'the' wall. As it happened, the wall that appeared in the video wasn't in the school at all, but no one wanted to hear that so in the end we just went along with it. It got so bad, though, that we introduced a protocol that the crews were not to be allowed on the premises. If they wanted to interview anyone from the school, it had to be done at the gate. The school was difficult enough run without constant interruptions to talk about Pink Floyd.

Being firmly on the media's radar, I was always extremely conscious of how certain incidents might play out in the wider world, which is something most heads don't have to consider. For example, I received an anonymous tip-off that one of our female teachers had a second job as a prostitute and a stripper, not to mention a serious cocaine habit. The complainant named the club where this woman allegedly worked and said it was despicable I had not done anything about it. The letter hinted that the story might be circulated to a wider audience.

This was a delicate situation on a number of levels. If the accusation was true, I couldn't very well leave this woman in charge of impressionable and often vulnerable children. Equally, if I didn't step carefully I might end up in court for constructive dismissal, in which case it would be all over the papers. Alternatively, if I did nothing, the matter might get spread all over the papers anyhow.

I consulted with John Challenor, who was always a source of wise counsel.

'Well, she is very attractive and the other staff have often commented on how well she dresses,' he said. 'Designer clothes, they reckon, not that I would notice these things. You'd need another income for that stuff when you're on a teacher's salary.'

'Yes, well, I can't really pull her into the office and ask her if she is a prostitute if I don't know if it is true,' I said.

'I could go to the club in the letter, check if it's true,' volunteered John. 'I'll just pop in, check if it's her and report back.'

John went to the club in London's Soho, along with Patrick, our new local community support police officer, who also volunteered his services. John returned to say he'd had a marvellous evening and our teacher was, indeed, a pole dancer, although there was absolutely no suggestion she offered more intimate services.

I had little choice but to confront her with the evidence. I called her into the head's office and showed her the letter. By breaking the news this way, which is my usual method with letters and emails to the head's office, I didn't need to paraphrase the contents. The evidence spoke for itself. She vehemently denied the accusation, claiming that she was actually a seamstress at the club making costumes. I didn't say she had been spotted stripping. I didn't have to. Just working in this club, in any capacity, would bring the school into disrepute. I told her she had a choice between the day job and the night time one. She resigned in a storm of protest, but she didn't seek any compensation or even take union advice, which spoke volumes. The story didn't, however, ever come out.

A big story that did have a huge and direct impact on the school was the bombings of 2005. On 7 July London was targeted by a series of terrorist attacks that rocked the capital. Coordinated suicide bombings on three underground trains and one double-decker bus killed fifty-two people and injured a further 700 in Britain's worst terrorist incident since Lockerbie in 1988. Communications were in chaos, the transport system ground to a halt and Londoners were terrified of further attacks. Islington Green was in between two of the four explosions.

It took a while for the news to filter through. In fact, to begin with, it felt like any other day. A few teachers hadn't made it in, but that wasn't completely out of the ordinary, even this far into the turnaround of the school. Then, at around 9.30am, the school office began getting anxious calls from parents. Once everyone had realised something serious was up, the change in atmosphere in the school was very noticeable. Anxious teachers abandoned all hope of conducting normal lessons and access to TVs was at a premium. Both adults and children stared in disbelief at the news that was unfolding on the small screen. Many of the kids were huddled around in small groups, talking in hushed voices, while some took themselves off to the loos to make surreptitious calls to their families on mobiles. When the mobile phone signal collapsed, a long queue formed outside the school office with people waiting to use the landline to call home.

We got a call from the emergency and disasters office at the local authority at around 10am, requesting that we kept the children in school until it could be verified that it was safe to leave. The sentiment was understandable, because at that chaotic stage there was a real fear of further attacks, but pupils were scared. Indeed, many of the streetwise kids who would normally be strutting down the corridor chanting 'we don't need no education' were particularly anxious. As I walked around the school, the feeling of panic was unmistakable.

I thought about the Tannoy system that I had consigned to the drawer soon after I joined the school and considered this might be one of the rare occasions where it actually might come in use as an effective means of communication.

As we dug it out of its resting place, I said a silent prayer it would still work after all this time. I needn't have worried. It was a pretty robust beast and had clearly survived years of abuse. I didn't have much time to think about what I was going to say; I just needed to reassure everyone that, although this was an extraordinary time, we had nothing to worry about.

Flicking the 'on' switch, I took a deep breath and began. 'I understand you will all be anxious today,' I said. 'I think everyone is aware that a terrorist bomb has been let off. You may have also heard that two of our teachers have been stranded near the incident, but I am assured as best I can that no one we know has been injured in the attack. In all likelihood nothing else is going to happen and we are all safe. So, I am going to ask you all to stay as calm as you can. The important thing to remember is you are all completely safe here in school.

'In the interests of safety I have been asked to keep you here until the local authorities have made sure everything is OK, but you will all be allowed to go home at the normal time. If, however, your parents are unable to get home because of problems with transport, you can stay here as long as necessary.'

I was told later that staff and pupils found the message really reassuring and the atmosphere in the school did calm down a little after I spoke. Indeed, it is a testament to the feeling of security that we had managed to create in the school that many pupils said they would prefer to stay anyhow because this was where they felt safe. They were allowed home at normal time, as I promised, and luckily we suffered no casualties among staff, parents or children.

As one of the schools in the thick of the chaos that day, we were asked by many media organisations for comment. In one of the many subsequent interviews, when I told the journalist about what went on in the school that day and about the reaction among the children, his eyes suddenly lit up.

'That would make an amazing play,' he declared.

Sure enough, the BBC commissioned a drama about the attacks that was aimed specifically at children. T*hat*

Summer Day focussed on how the bombings affected pupils at an ethnically mixed North London secondary school and it was filmed over two weeks at Islington Green itself. A number of the staff and children even appeared as extras. Shown on the first anniversary of the atrocity, it depicted the events through the eyes of six fictitious pupils. Material for the drama, written by Clive Bradley and directed by Jon East, was gathered from interviews with more than 700 kids from London schools, including a large number from Islington Green.

I agreed to the filming not just because of the small donation the production company made to the school coffers, which was always handy, but also because it was a great experience for the children, following the horrors of that day. I was also sending a message to both children and parents about how proud I was of the way everyone had behaved under the most trying and intense circumstances.

Chapter nine

WORKING WITH PARENTS

Working with the families that sent their children to us was an important element in the turnaround of Islington Green. We were at the centre of several large estates that were dominated by around twenty-five large families, many of whom had links with one another. Many of the parents weren't working and a number derived at least part of their income from the black economy. There must have been some fairly successful enterprises in this arena too, judging by the size of the TVs in some homes, which also boasted some pretty swanky fixtures and fittings. That's not to mention the caravans on the coast and the villas in Spain that some of the kids openly boasted about. Grandparents played an important part in family life and in around a third of cases they took on the role of carer. The family structure was solid, which is a good thing, but woe betide any hapless head who fell foul of what families expected from their school.

Working with parents

While I was all for establishing a happy and productive working relationship with the Islington Green community, doing so was often not that straight forward. Indeed, with some families it was well-nigh impossible.

When Arash joined Islington Green in Year 7, I was already prepared for potential conflict. The lad had two older brothers, Baki and Faruk in Years 10 and 11, and the pair were violent and disruptive. I had already held a number of meetings with their parents and they hadn't gone well. Both the mother and father were hostile and uncooperative and there were rumours that the family had a high position in the Turkish criminal gangs that populated the area. They certainly had an arrogant and dismissive air and insisted on a Turkish translator for all of our discussions, although I suspected they could speak English perfectly well. Most of our meetings ended with the father shouting an endless stream of incomprehensible abuse at me while wagging his finger inches from my face.

The translator, who was one of our teachers, would helpfully summarise the gist of what the parent said.

'He is very unhappy,' she'd say with a shrug. 'He doesn't agree with you.'

I had sort of picked that up, I thought irritably.

It was apparent straight away that Arash was struggling. He had a very low IQ and was unable to keep up with even the most basic lessons. He clearly needed help and I was a little surprised this hadn't been flagged up by his primary school, although, if his previous teachers had met the parents too, it was probably understandable they had left the problem for someone else to deal with.

Arash was an obvious candidate for our Learning Zone, which provided special education for youngsters who needed more help. It was the right thing to do. The trouble was, doing the right thing and satisfying his parents were at opposite ends of the scale. The parents hated the idea of their youngest son going into the Learning Zone and demanded a meeting straight away.

'You are labelling him,' stormed the father via the translator.

'I am not,' I replied, pausing to let the translator do his job. 'We can't meet his needs in a regular class and it is in his best interests to get some additional help now.'

As soon as the translator had finished, Arash's father exploded. Speaking rapidly in a deep, angry voice, he vented his fury as his wife nodded in agreement.

I held up my hand to the translator. I didn't need the full text of the diatribe. Slowly and deliberately I began to explain the ideas and techniques behind the Learning Zone. It was hard going, not least because at the end of each translated sentence the Turkish couple would vigorously shake their heads and say 'olmaz', which I now knew to mean an emphatic 'no'. They made it quite clear they didn't agree with me and were unlikely to ever come close to doing so either.

At long last I had had enough.

'I have heard what you are saying and understand your concerns, but I have to tell you that this is something we don't need your agreement for,' I said. 'It is what we are going to do. If you really object, you can take Arash elsewhere and that is your prerogative. As I have said repeatedly, we cannot meet his needs in a regular class.'

The parents wouldn't let it drop and over the next few weeks I received a stream of legal letters as well as a visit from a community advocate. Finally, by way of compromise, we agreed to put Arash into the Learning Zone for 50 per cent of the school day and to let him join regular classes for the rest of the time. It was a messy solution and I wasn't happy with it, but right then it seemed the best way to deal with something that was already taking up a disproportionate amount of my time.

I sensed the episode wasn't yet over and, sure enough, within weeks it took a decidedly worse turn. Arash got into a heated dispute with one of the teachers of the regular classes. He had been using his mobile phone in the classroom, the teacher had tried to stop him and he had refused. The argument very quickly escalated and after the teacher demanded the boy hand over the phone there was some sort of scuffle and Arash got a small scratch to his hand. It was completely inexcusable that the teacher had engaged with the boy physically, particularly when I had repeatedly warned the team that touching was never acceptable. However, right then, my greater concern was about where this was heading. Sure enough, the next time Arash saw the teacher, he punched him in a brutal and unprovoked attack.

Enough was enough. There was no way Arash could be allowed to stay in mainstream lessons after that. It just wasn't safe for my team. Despite protests from his parents, we arranged for the boy to join a separate educational arrangement outside school. The alternative site was a privately run venture on Islington High Street and offered a range of activities and one-to-one tutoring. I had previously set up a retainer arrangement with the person who ran the venture and would occasionally send over kids who simply couldn't, or wouldn't, fit in with the main school regardless of our best efforts.

Arash was there for one day before he punched a tutor. By then I had no choice but to permanently exclude him. That is when things really kicked off. In no time at all a legal letter arrived informing me and the school that Arash's parents were taking us to a tribunal. They accused the school and local authority of making inadequate provision for their son's education and were seeking compensation in the region of £400,000. The move heralded an intense period of activity with many hours spent producing detailed documentary proof to rebuff each one of the claims. What made it all the more stressful was that it was clear from the very beginning that the local authority was in a real panic. Their first instinct was to settle because they were fearful of being landed with an enormous bill for damages, whereas I was prepared to fight the family all the way. After all, as I had repeatedly tried to explain to Arash's parents, I had only ever tried to act in the boy's best interests.

The tribunal itself was pretty nerve wracking. It was held over three days at the centre in Canonbury, Islington, and the room was packed with interpreters, lawyers, community representatives and numerous people from the local authority. As I looked around at everyone, I had to remind myself that we had done all we could and probably a great deal more than many schools would have done faced with the same set of circumstances. I had tried repeatedly to engage with Arash's parents but they had been resistant to all my efforts. All I had to do was to convince the tribunal of the facts.

After going through all the evidence, the tribunal panel agreed that we had acted reasonably. The only area where the local authority did come under some criticism was for the fact that no one had spotted that this child required additional help earlier on, while he was still at primary school. If his needs had been dealt with earlier, the outcome may not have been the same, which was a fair point. The parents were awarded nominal compensation of a couple of thousand pounds for the primary school's oversight. Looking back at the episode, I am still convinced I did the right thing, although I also believe that whatever I did the outcome would probably have been the same. Arash was always going to follow in the footsteps of his older brothers and indeed is now in prison doing time for a particularly nasty stabbing incident.

As Arash's story shows, it isn't always easy to get parents on side. Although this is an extreme example, this gulf between parents and the school was by no means isolated.

Finding a way to work with parents was one of the key items of my initial plan when I joined Islington Green and something that was a priority on an ongoing basis.

At Islington Green many parents came from quite challenging backgrounds themselves. A lot of them were on the edge of handling life in general, let alone anything out of the ordinary. One of the main reasons I wanted to get rid of the regime of rampant exclusions, apart from the fact teachers were becoming trigger happy with them and they served no real purpose, is they drove parents mad, and quite understandably so in most cases. It was far more effective all round to run an exclusion room and the feedback from parents on this initiative was positive.

My philosophy is that schools need to stop treating parents like the enemy. This syndrome is invariably found in weak and failing schools, where heads adopt an ostrich-like strategy of hiding away from anyone who might ask awkward questions. In one particular school I was aware of, though thankfully not Islington Green, the head had a line on the floor in reception that parents were not permitted to cross. If parents (while sticking to their side of the divide) made an enquiry at the office and it was referred on to the head, she'd never reply. She wouldn't go out on the gate and parents rarely caught a glimpse of her at all. Hardly surprisingly, they formed a view that the head wasn't interested and didn't care.

It is very much the head's job to manage the message that goes out to parents as much as the one that goes out to students. A school is, or at least should be, a big part of the community. A school should be clear and consistent in its messages and be prepared to deliver them with conviction.

One of my first acts was to change the way we interacted with parents. Previously, they were treated something like the following. When anything went awry, parents would march up to the school, storm into reception and demand to see the head immediately. The startled receptionist would naturally call through to the head's office, only to be told they were too busy to see anyone. The poor receptionist then conveyed this unsatisfactory message to the parent, winding them up still further. She then further exacerbated an already terrible situation by making a rapid succession of calls to the deputy head, the head of year and perhaps even a form teacher, working down the chain of command and delivering the same negative outlook each time. By this stage, the irate parent would be at exploding point and an already bad situation was made much, much worse.

I immediately signalled a new regime where, if it was humanly possible, I would always make time to speak to parents, either face to face or over the phone. As a head I was always sure to be highly visible and would be at the school gate as often as I could. It is an easy thing to do and ensures everyone knows who you are. Even if I didn't get to speak to everyone, parents knew I was the head and could see me. People felt emboldened to come up to me and most of the time they asked pretty trivial things, for example about what was happening to the annual school trip to so and so, or something else that was equally simple to answer in a few words. That was fine. Before they may have written in about it, but now they could ask their question and get an answer quickly. The knock-on effect of a head's presence at the gate is that everyone tends to behave better. If no one is out there it is quite easy for others to begin to feel that area of the school is their territory. It is but a small step for it to be taken over by the local community and kids rather than being controlled by the head. In my opinion, ten minutes spent on the gate is ten minutes well spent.

Only once did the strategy backfire. One afternoon a student who had been excluded under the previous regime came up behind me and gave me a right old whack to the back of the head. I didn't even see him coming and only found out who had attacked me some time later. That said, the rest of the time, it was fine.

If I spoke to parents over the phone, my number-one rule was to agree with them, which was something that used to drive the team close around me mad, and it took me a long time to convince them I was doing the right thing. My reasoning was that, by the time parents got to the stage of calling me, they were usually pretty agitated. Acknowledging that they may have a point, which they invariably did in some way or another, takes the edge off things. This isn't to say that I didn't direct them back to the appropriate channels, but by listening to their views I could change their perspective entirely.

One day, for example, a parent approached me because

she was worried her child had special needs but the school was falling a long way short. She was clearly very upset, but most troubling for me was her assertion that she believed the school was pretending there was no issue at all.

She said, 'I am convinced they have been giving him false grades to make things look better than they really are. I've asked them again and again to take steps to apply for a statement of special needs, but they are really dragging their feet.

'I get the feeling that if I don't keep on and on at it nothing will be done. My son will never have his needs met. It is terrible.'

Very often, in a situation like this, professionals will parrot back non-committal nonsense about 'looking into things' or 'passing it on to the appropriate person' or some such excuse to fob a caller off. They may even try to hide behind the assertion that they are entirely the wrong person to call. I'm sure it is down to a fear of ending up in a tribunal if they 'admit' anything, but in my view this is completely the wrong tactic. It is far better to show a parent you understand where they are coming from and even go one step further by thanking them for raising the issue. This is certainly the tactic I employed in this case.

I told the parent, 'I completely agree with you. It does sound like something has gone very wrong here and I will look into it straight away.

'I am very glad you've got in touch with me. It is very helpful when people highlight where there may be issues in our policies because it means we can make things right in the future. Thank you very much.'

Addressing problems like this defuses the tension and makes things easier. Small things like listening to parents' complaints and asking parents what they want the school to do make a tremendous difference. Even if a problem can't be solved immediately, things will be a lot easier to handle if everyone is calm and the parent is not jumping up and down in a rage. I did my best to keep my language positive to give them confidence something will be done and deliberately used words such as 'I will' instead of vague reassurances such as 'I could' or 'I don't think we can do that.' I also tried to drop some of the formalities and spoke to them like regular people rather than addressing them in the manner of a corporate stiff who can't wait to shuffle the problem on to someone else. A little familiarity, even levity when appropriate, can go a long way to getting a parent on side.

In considering my own phone manner I got to thinking more about the usual contact parents got from the school. Inexplicably, many teachers were in the habit of regularly ringing up families to tell them how out of control their kids were: 'Oh, hello Mrs Smith. I thought I had better tell you that Billy was up to his old tricks in English today.'

Hardly surprisingly, parents were fed up to the back teeth with the school. They were sick of hearing about it. I had a slight suspicion that teachers were making the calls to get their own back at kids like Billy because they couldn't control them, but either way the calls were helping no one.

I had a light-bulb moment when I was talking to an angry parent. She had come to see me to complain about the treatment of her son.

'I never ever hear a good thing about Jonah,' she said. 'I dread picking up the phone these days.'

She had a point too. We were perpetuating the bad image of the school with every phone call we made. I decided then and there on a new policy. At the next staff meeting I told the team that for every 'bad' call that was made home a teacher would have to balance it with three 'good' calls. We would put in place a new system of positive calls.

I said, 'We should be saying, "Hello Mrs Jones. I just wanted to let you know Daryl has been brilliant today. I know you usually get negative calls, but today he has been great. Make sure you praise him."'

I knew very well that if we did this the next day Daryl would come in grinning all over his face: 'Miss Barr, mum is so pleased she let me have an hour extra on my PlayStation.'

Instantly his behaviour will improve. It is not rocket science.

The staff were pretty reluctant when I first floated the idea. They found it hard to see past the extra work it meant.

'It's only going to take a few minutes of your time, but the upside to this sort of positive communication will last for weeks,' I told them.

To ease the transition, I arranged training for the teachers in how to tackle the calls. Then, I instigated a system where, on a department-by-department basis, the teachers would all sit down together to phone parents. I suggested that the calls home became part of the positive discipline system. If a child got X number of ticks on the board, they would get a call home to say how well they had done.

Although the team was reluctant and needed constant badgering to make the calls, there was clear evidence they had an effect. Alison was one teacher in particular who was having real problems exerting control. The kids were throwing things at her and being very unpleasant.

'Find something that a few of them have done well and make the call,' I urged.

Alison looked pretty cynical that it would have any effect and was probably struggling with the idea that she could find anything at all that any of her class did well. However, she agreed to give it a go.

A few days later, Alison came running up to me in the corridor. 'It is a miracle, a miracle!' she began. 'They are behaving beautifully.'

Interestingly, though, this teacher didn't keep up the calls home. The children were good for about four weeks after the initial calls and after that went straight back into their old habits. I had to remind her that, for positive communication to work effectively, it has to be regular and systematic. She had to keep on top of the calls for them to have a long-lasting effect.

Working with parents

As the project to turn around Islington Green progressed, I constantly came back to what a big issue language is in schools. I don't mean the somewhat colourful words that many of the children bandy around; I mean the way teachers communicate with both the children and their parents. At Islington Green, teachers were too prone to falling back on vague or over-exaggerated phrases to describe incidents and it was driving parents mad.

In my regular tours of the school I began to collect words and phrases that any head should be wary about. First among them had to be any sentence that incorporated the word 'failed', as in 'Will *failed* to attend the lesson' or 'James *failed* to produce his assignment.'

The alternative was to talk in lazy generalities, such as, 'Kelly is *constantly* disruptive.'

These are all highly emotive expressions and instantly label the child. No wonder the parents got angry. It was not a problem unique to Islington Green either. Indeed, my most memorable instance of this poor use of language came when I was a deputy head working at Alec Hunter. The redoubtable Head of Upper School there was a lady called Heather Williams. She was larger than life in size, personality and presence. I used to joke with her that when she walked down the corridors the walls would shake and the classrooms would darken as she passed. No one would cross Heather.

She burst into my office one day, clearly very flustered.

'Mr Averre-Beeson, come with me,' she commanded, without any polite preamble.

No one argued with Heather, so I got to my feet and followed her out into the corridor.

'What's the problem?' I asked as I hurried along in her wake.

'Duane is causing a riot,' she said, without a backward glance.

'Really? A riot? What happened?'

'Mr Haigh has been in and can't sort it out and so has Mrs Whittaker. I went in and he ignored me.'

Blimey, I thought, this must be serious. Not only did no one dare confront Heather but defying Steve Haigh, the six-foot Head of Humanities, was a brave move. I didn't have a chance to press further to find out the cause of the riot because we had reached the classroom. Heather dramatically threw open the door and strode in. I followed her in and my eyes did a rapid sweep of the class. Most of the boys and girls were sitting at their desks, their faces a curious mixture of fear, curiosity and sheer delight at this episode. My eyes were drawn to a boy at the back of the class: Duane. To my amazement, he was sat back in his chair, arms folded casually behind his head, legs up on the table in front of him. His expression was relaxed and content and he looked rather like he was chilling by the side of the pool on holiday.

'What happened?' I asked, turning to Stella Whittaker.

'We were doing a test as part of the GCSE coursework and, as you know, we need to do these tests in controlled conditions. Duane threw his pencil across the room in frustration,' she said, articulating the word frustration as though it was quite the most appalling emotion she had ever had the misfortune to experience.

I looked questioningly over at Duane, who was staring back at me. He gave a brief nod to indicate his agreement with the charge.

'What happened then?'

'I said, "Duane, come and pick up the pencil," and he wouldn't.'

I paused because I sensed there would be more.

Stella continued: 'I said to him, "Duane, if you don't come and pick up the pencil you will not be allowed to complete this task and if you don't complete this task you won't be able to do your GCSE. If you don't do your GCSEs, you won't be able to join the sixth form. If you don't pass your A Levels, you won't go to university and you won't get a job. You'll never have any money."

'Do you know what he said to me? He said, "All through not picking up my pencil miss?"'

Stella crossed her arms defiantly and her chin jutted out in an expression of utter disgust.

I looked over and the pencil was still lying on the floor in front of Duane's desk. I had to shake an image that crept into my brain where the pencil had a thick line drawn around it, like a murder victim on one of those dreadful seventies TV detective dramas. It was obvious everyone was waiting for me to react and I could feel every eye in the room staring at me.

Stepping forward, I bent down and picked up the pencil.

'Duane, come with me,' I said, putting the pencil on the desk and stepping back to let him walk in front of me.

He got up quite happily and we went straight to my office. He still seemed as relaxed as ever and slightly nonplussed about what had just happened. As I dialled his mother's number I looked at him sitting in the chair in front of me. He was a good-looking lad with long, dark hair and a pleasant, if wilful, personality. Duane's confidence and self-esteem were strong and not much seemed to get him down. He was a bright boy too and knew he could run rings around most people.

'Ah, hello Mrs Roberts, it is Mr Averre-Beeson. I have Duane in my office again.'

A long sigh. 'What's happened?'

'I'm afraid I am going to have to send Duane home.'

'What for?'

'He has defied every member of staff and every level of authority in the school.'

'My God, what did he do?'

'He defied Mrs Whittaker and he defied Mrs Williams…'

'He defied Mrs Williams?' Her voice was slow and shocked. 'Really? I can't believe it. What was it all about?'

'He threw a pencil across the room…'

I didn't get any further before Mrs Roberts exploded.

'You are excluding him for throwing a pencil across the room?'

As she was saying it, I thought, she's right. This is

ridiculous. This mother was echoing back to me what I had been thinking all along. Yes, Duane was deliberately winding us all up, but we were dancing to his tune. I didn't send him home, but I learned a big lesson that day about the power of over-exaggerated words and phrases and how damaging they can be both at school and in relations with parents. It is no wonder they get exasperated when they can clearly see it is the teacher and the school that generate the problem. If the emotive language is dropped, parent–teacher relations will improve at a stroke.

Chapter ten

SELLING ISLINGTON GREEN

It was vitally important to improve relations with parents at Islington Green too. When I joined the school it consistently didn't feature as first choice for any parent. Tony Blair was not alone in not wanting his child anywhere near the place. There had been a number of strange and wonderful initiatives to address this in the past, all geared to a desire to attract 'better' pupils. The most misguided of these ideas was, in my opinion, the introduction of an elite stream for able and middle-class children. A promise was made to prospective parents that these children would receive extra attention and would be protected all the way through their secondary education. They may as well have stuck a big 'hit me' sign on these poor kids. They were, quite naturally, permanently terrified to be singled out and most of their intellectual energies were deployed in finding places to hide from the other, less privileged, children. It was unfair on them and unfair on the other 80 per cent of the pupils, who were perfectly good kids with a range of abilities who didn't deserve to be singled out for the slush pile. I got rid of that system as soon as I arrived.

The challenge, as I saw it, was how to make Islington Green the number-one choice for the local community, regardless of class or ability. It seemed to me the only rational policy was to make the school the best it could be for the largest number of people. Even with the improvements we had already made, this was quite a challenge.

I learned very early on in my career as a head that if there is a community of 1,050 kids there is always going to be someone, somewhere not far away, who is very cross with the school. There will be a brick thrown through a window at the end of term, or an ongoing problem with traffic at school pick-up or drop-off time, or unrest about large groups of children hanging around where they shouldn't be. Quite often, heads get complaints about issues like these and don't deal with them very well. The problem will fester and add to an already negative opinion of the school in the local community. Over time it does some real damage.

Sorting out our relations with the local community and, of course, prospective parents was high on my action list. At the simplest level I made a big point of answering my phone to talk to complainants directly or phoning someone up when they had left an irate message. At Islington Green we had an ongoing issue with the kids throwing rubbish over the fence into the private gardens around the school. Some of our elderly neighbours were also quite anxious about the rowdy behaviour of our kids when they walked to and from school.

I took a few minutes out of my day and went out of school to see the affected people. I let them vent a little about 'kids of today' and had a chuckle to myself when one of the elderly gentlemen concerned moved seamlessly from complaining into telling me how he used to go to my school as a nipper and was a 'right little tearaway'. I assured them I was always available and to their visible surprise I gave them my mobile number.

'Call me anytime you get a problem,' I said. I meant it too.

A short while later, I was in New York at a conference when my mobile rang. I was in my hotel, because it was 5am, but I was awake.

'I don't know if you remember me, but it's Fred from Raleigh Street…' began the voice at the other end.

'Yes, I do remember you, Fred. How are you?'

'Well, I'm all right, but those kids have been up to their tricks again. They've been throwing stuff at my roof.'

'Oh, I am very sorry to hear that. What time is it at the moment, Fred? I'm in New York right now you see.'

'It's 1pm. I am sorry to disturb you,' he said, his voice now faltering a little.

'No, no, not at all. I'll get right on to it. Thanks for taking the trouble to call me.'

The moment I clicked off the phone, I called Anne, who was in her office in Islington Green. She did sound a little surprised to hear from me. I asked her to get one of the deputies to sort the matter out and then to pop round to Raleigh Street to make sure everything was OK. The problem was dealt with quickly and our neighbours thought I, and more importantly the school, was wonderful.

Being accessible means you have to be just that. There is nothing worse than someone who says 'call me, anytime, I will sort it out' and then doesn't take the call or takes no action. It is not that difficult to do either. I only had a handful of calls from our neighbours the whole time I was at that school, but the act of giving them my number and then sorting out their problems made a huge difference. It was a useful first step in changing the previously negative views of the school of the local community too.

One of my early acts in transforming Islington Green into a more attractive option was to introduce full school uniforms in January 2003. The team had raised the problem with uniforms very early on. The kids from Year 9 upwards didn't wear uniforms at all and the ones in the years below had a very loose interpretation of the admittedly vague dress code. Even though there was a widespread desire for change, when I raised the issue, many of the staff and even some people on the SLT were highly resistant to the idea of introducing a formal uniform for everyone.

'They won't wear blazers,' they said.

'You'd be surprised,' I said.

'Isn't lilac a bit, well…' began Ken Muller.

'Feminine?' I said. 'Really? You of all people, labelling a person by the colour they wear? Should we really be having this conversation?'

Of course he, or indeed anyone else, couldn't really object, so the children were measured up and the aubergine blazers ordered. On the day the boxes of blazers arrived and the children were told to go to the hall to collect them, there were queues around the building. They loved the idea.

'Look at me, sir, it looks like we're a proper school now,' grinned Jason, a Year 11, adjusting his lapels as he walked past and giving a cheeky dip of his head. I couldn't help smiling. He'd hit the nail on the head.

One of the biggest concerns of the uniform detractors was that outsiders would be able to easily identify Islington Green pupils whenever they did something wrong outside the school. With this in mind, I spoke at a series of assemblies about the responsibility that came with the new uniform.

'Be proud of your blazers,' I told the children. 'Everyone will know who you are now, so that means you need to behave outside school too.'

Then, the most incredible thing happened. Almost overnight we started to get letters and phone calls saying how well behaved Islington Green pupils were outside the school. In the past a thousand kids would leave school and perhaps half a dozen would get up to no good, shoplifting or throwing stones. People would see kids doing something they shouldn't be doing, put two and two together and naturally assume they were from Islington Green, even though sometimes they weren't. They barely noticed the other 900-plus kids who went home nicely, chatting among themselves or swapping football cards. Now, of course, they could identify our children easily. Locals, and among them prospective parents, could see standards were rising.

In a stroke of good fortune, one of those locals was *The Sunday Times'* educational correspondent, Geraldine Hackett. She noticed the purple blazers going by and wrote a story about them. Then, in a further lucky break, the story was followed up by the *Daily Mail*, although the paper couldn't resist having a pop at me for being a 'liberal head teacher'. It implied I was putting thugs in pink blazers, which was I believe partly a misinterpretation of a joke I had made in the school newsletter. I had quipped that the kids needn't worry: the blazers were not pink, they were actually aubergine. Still, all good publicity and all that. The message was getting through. Islington Green was changing and it was hard for parents to ignore that.

Now Islington Green kids were so identifiable, I also needed to do something concrete about the fights that regularly erupted in and immediately around the school. I was realistic. I was never going to stop them altogether, but, if they did erupt, I could at least encourage the children to take them a very long way away from school premises. I spoke about it at the Year 11 assembly and then invited small groups of the likeliest lads to speak to me in my office. I didn't read them the riot act though. That would never have worked and may even have had the opposite effect. Instead, I appealed to their sense of pride in the school, which by that time was beginning to emerge.

'Do you know what is wrong about this school?' I asked each group. 'Everyone on the outside thinks it is all about fighting.'

A few of the boys sniggered at this.

'This doesn't matter to me,' I said, enjoying the look of surprise that flashed across a few faces. 'I'll be the head of another school one day. My family already lives a long way away. The only person who should truly care about the reputation of your school is you.'

Looking around the room, I picked out one of the leaders.

'Ben, you like a fight, don't you?'

'Oh yes sir, I like a fight.'

'Well, the rest of us don't want your fight. We care about the reputation of the school. Take your fight away.'

'What sir? Are you saying it's OK to fight?'

'No. What I am saying is: if you fight in and around the school, you won't be here for long. However, if you take the fight away, far, far away, then I won't know anything about it.'

Cue knowing nods from the assembled group.

A short while later, someone obviously decided it was time to challenge my strength of feeling over fighting.

Staff got wind of the fact a fight was being planned for the end of the school day and someone tipped me off. I went straight to the staff room and addressed everyone there.

'I'd like some volunteers,' I announced to the less than impressed throng. 'I have been told that there is to be a fight this afternoon at the close of play. We are going to have to be a bit brave about this, but my hunch is the kids won't want to get into a scuffle with adults. If we show up in enough force, link arms and gently usher them out of the school I think they will get the message. Is anyone with me on this?'

Incredibly, around twenty of the younger teachers stepped forward to join me.

'This is crazy,' said Jane Fielding, feisty as ever. 'But it might just work.'

It did too. The kids looked surprised, but they allowed themselves to be moved on by my band of brave teachers. After that, we had a routine. Every time we got a sniff of a fight, we'd turn out in force and usher the perpetrators off the premises. Over time it got easier and easier and gradually we got down to virtually no fights on or around the site.

Following the success with the anti-fighting initiative and the uniforms, I thought it was high time we came out from behind closed doors and started showing the community and, of course, prospective parents, how proud we were about the changes at Islington Green.

There is a natural tendency in difficult schools to

hide away and attempt to keep things locked down. The flawed reasoning is that, if parents can't see how bad things are, they won't really believe it. It doesn't work and parents instinctively know the reason they are being kept away is because they won't like what they see.

Islington Green's annual open-day event was a classic example. When I joined, the open day was, in fact, an open evening and the school struggled to get even sixty families to attend. Not surprisingly, it was an awful occasion, with the small number of families rattling around the vast, imposing and empty school. Equally unsurprisingly, most people left our open evenings with an appalling impression of Islington Green and the poor teaching team was exhausted and depressed after achieving nothing but perpetuating the negative image of the school. Not only did the events serve no purpose, they actually made a bad situation worse.

'What we need to do is have an open day,' I told the SLT during our weekly meeting. 'In the day time, while the children are here.'

To a man and woman, they looked horrified.

'We can't have people coming here during the day,' Angela exclaimed. 'We've improved, but daytime in the school is still not for the faint-hearted. There is always something to surprise you.'

'Of course we can,' I said. 'Most of what goes on in the school is fine and we will manage the rest. We won't take anyone where we know there is going to be a problem and, if something does go wrong, let's deal with it and show the parents how well we deal with it.'

I reasoned that the open approach would be much better on a number of levels. For a start, it would show we had nothing to hide. Indeed, we were proud of our school. Plus, we were likely to get a much better turnout during the day. Many of our target families didn't want to go out in the evenings to view their child's prospective school. They might be tied up looking after other children, settling down for a night in front of the TV or just not bothered. Invite them out during the day, though, and things would be different. If they were working, they'd probably relish the opportunity to get a few hours off with the perfect excuse that they 'had' to visit their kid's new school. Families tied up with other children were much more likely to be able to make other arrangements during the day too.

The SLT was still doubtful, but I pressed the point. Over the next few months we instigated a programme to transform the school's appearance. In addition to the earlier lilac revamp of the corridors, artists were commissioned to do themed murals there too. There was a Shakespeare theme outside the English rooms, rockets next to the science labs and so on. A short video was produced extolling the virtues of Islington Green and after some discussion we decided we'd show it at the end of the tour so parents would go away with a nice image of the school imprinted in their minds.

On the first open day, we had 300 people due in. We timed the event carefully, holding it before first break so the children were in their classes and everyone was calm. We also agreed a pre-determined route for the parental tours. There would be sweepers out front who were under the iron control of Hannah, who was great at this sort of thing. Their job was to clear up any trouble spots before the tour groups passed by. We agreed a code whereby if a teacher kept their classroom door open it was fine to show parents what was happening in the class inside. If the door was shut we would rapidly move the visitors along.

Before we let the first parents in, I gathered the team together for a last-minute pep talk.

I said, 'I know some of you are still nervous about today, but I know it will go a lot better than any of you imagine. We have come a long way and I think we should give ourselves more credit for it. Yes, it is a risk, but it is a controlled and calculated risk. I am certain that our visitors will be pleasantly surprised by what they find here. They will arrive expecting to see some sort of chaotic nuthouse and will go away with the impression of a well-run, happy school.'

I paused, waiting for the usual smattering of surreptitiously exchanged glances between the most cynical teachers. I noticed to my satisfaction that they didn't happen.

'My prediction is the children will rise to the occasion,' I went on. 'We all know they calm down when visitors are here. Ninety-nine per cent of the time they are proud of the school and like showing it off to strangers. They know it is in all our interests to make a good impression.'

My mind flicked back to the Ofsted inspection in early 2003. I had done the speech in assembly that all heads do. The one where the head says, 'I know you all think it is an inspection of the teachers and me, but actually this is all about you. I am not going to be in this job forever, but this school will stick with you for the rest of your life. When you write Islington Green on a job application in fifteen years' time, is the employer going to think, "Islington Green, I wouldn't touch them with a barge pole"? Or are they going to think, "Well, that is a good school"? This is all about you and your future,' I told the kids.

I smiled to myself when I pictured walking down the corridor with the inspector. It seemed so long ago now. We were behind a group of three of the most bolshy girls in the school: Tara, Ayeshan and Yasmin.

'Oh, this is such a lovely school,' cooed Yasmin in a very loud voice.

'Yeah, it didn't use to be very nice,' agreed Tara loudly, with a very obvious glance behind her.

'Now it is really epic,' giggled Ayeshan.

The inspector glanced over at me and smiled.

'Did you do the usual assembly?' he asked quietly.

'Yes, is it that obvious?'

He nodded but was still smiling. We both knew that, even in their emotionally unintelligent way, these girls had sent out a big signal. They had respect for the school and wanted to do the right thing. I was confident this behaviour would be repeated for the open days too.

Sure enough, the children were well behaved and the teachers really upped their game too. Everyone felt a sense of pride in showing off their school and it became a virtuous circle because prospective parents were inspired by the positive emotion. Buoyed by the reaction, we held more events. Over time, as the open days became more successful, we started to get more people coming to them.

The success of the open days was reflected in the figures. From no first choices at all when I arrived, we reached a tipping point by 2005 where Islington Green was the first choice for more than half the children who started in Year 7. Instead of shunning the school, parents were now actively choosing to send their children there. It had a positive knock-on effect on behaviour, commitment and, in a very short space of time, results too. In my first year there, results rose from just 11 per cent A* to C to 27 per cent, and by 2004 they were almost lapping themselves at the 50 per cent mark.

Although I could see the figures rising steadily, there was one particular moment I knew we had truly made a big leap forward. The TES produced a cartoon depicting Cherie Blair bringing her son Leo to Islington Green. We had gone from being the school famously rejected by the Blairs to one outsiders reckoned was OK after all.

Following the success of the open day and buoyed by the positive comments elsewhere, I figured that, when it comes to making a good impression on parents and the immediate community, is it is never too early to start. I decided to begin making a big point of getting to know the heads of all the local primary schools. I began a rolling programme of going out to see them at every opportunity so I could talk positively about the senior school. I asked them whether I could take assemblies on the grounds that the head is the most important face the kids are going to get to know and, if they already knew me, it would make their transition a lot easier.

I still felt we could go further in building links with the feeder schools and luckily I got to know a fantastically creative woman called Margy Knutson. This was the time when the Labour government was spending money hand over fist on education and had created what it called an Education Action Zone (EAZ) in Islington. Margy had been put in charge with a £1–2 million budget to make things happen. Islington Green was in one of twenty-five EAZs, which covered clusters of around twenty schools. There were usually two or three secondary schools in each cluster, and in our case the group contained us and Highbury Grove with the rest being made up of nearby primary and nursery schools. The idea was to link difficult, or poorly performing, schools with the local community, parents and local businesses to try to foster the ethos of learning. When I met Margy, a true Islingtonite, she was based in a tiny loft office above a garage.

Most of the schools in the area saw Margy's work as something they wanted to avoid. True, she did have a slightly 'creative' approach, some might even say wacky, but I could see what she was trying to do and fully supported the idea of a closer integration with primary schools. I offered her an office beside mine within Islington Green and a space on the SLT.

Margy introduced a number of innovative ideas, such as super-learning days, which were run in partnership with primaries. These were fun days where the aim was to pack a lot of learning into a short space of time. So, for example, we'd introduce a new learning technique by bringing in a troupe of jugglers. Or we'd get performers in to explain Pythagoras' theorem using plastic cups. We set a series of motivating challenges that were well away from the usual teaching day.

Margy also brought in a system where some of our teachers in IT and PE went out to the other schools to run classes and clubs. The integration between the schools in the borough increased exponentially and attitudes of potential pupils and their parents improved markedly. This again contributed to the number of times Islington Green appeared as a first-choice option.

Inevitably, many of the local school heads we worked with were always a little sceptical. On more than one occasion I was asked, 'What happens to the kids we send you? They leave here all fresh faced and willing to please and within months they have changed completely and are getting kicked out for being troublemakers.'

They had a point too and the issue had been mentioned by a number of parents as well. Islington Green had a problem that is common to many of the London boroughs and indeed other cities, and that was how to successfully manage the transition from primary to secondary school. As Tony Blair proved, while many middle-class parents are prepared to commit to local primaries, they often choose to go outside the area for secondary education.

This was a question that many educators other than myself had wrestled with. And, if parents did send their children to our schools, there was the ever-present problem of transition, which is universal. It seemed no one had come up with the perfect answer to how to ease the passage of children from the cosseted, protective and disciplined cocoon of their junior school, where they might be based in just one room with one teacher, into an environment where there are hundreds of other children, a large number of subjects (each with its own teacher) and a need to travel a great distance between lessons. The transition affects children in different ways, but very often they get completely distracted and their grades go downhill fast.

I'd been mulling over the problem for some months when Peter suggested I took a trip to America to see how that country's Charter schools work. The idea, which had been introduced by Bill Clinton, had been hugely successful and particularly effective at integrating younger children into senior schools and inspiring them to do great things. The discussion about Charter schools was part of a wider debate about the value of the new academy system that was bubbling away in Westminster at that time, but it seemed to me it would be an opportunity missed if I didn't see what could be done.

My trip to a Charter school was a revelation. There were just 100 places at this tiny school in the Bronx, and the kids who got in (via a lottery system) were so hyped up and highly motivated it was clear they were going to get results.

Cynics might have laughed at the school's head for his motivational pronouncements, such as 'Give me an E grader and I will give you an A grader,' but I believed him. He had perfected a highly personalised approach and I had another one of those light-bulb moments.

Inspired by the American Charter school example, I formed an idea to set up a highly personalised school-within-a school, ring-fencing Year 7s from the rest of the school. Under the initiative, which I called Charter 7, children starting Islington Green would have their classrooms together, along the same corridor, and teachers would come to them rather than expecting them to trek between classrooms. The Year 7s would be subject to different hours from the rest of the school and the curriculum reduced to focus on literacy and numeracy.

The idea was to replicate, at least in part, some of the small-community, family atmosphere the children had experienced at primary school. By giving them separate facilities and lunch and break times, as well as the same teacher for most of the day, the transition would be much easier to manage. Children would feel more safe and secure and parents felt less nervous about the move to senior school.

I floated the idea to the SLT midway through the summer term of 2004 and said I wanted to introduce it at the beginning of the autumn term in September. Angela and Emma, who had been with me on the trip to see the Charter school in New York, were enthusiastic. I expected Hannah to be the most resistant. She was in charge of timetables and was already a substantial way through the one for the following year.

'The changes will require a little building work and some substantial rejigging of timetables, but I do believe it is perfectly possible to achieve it in the three months we have before the beginning of the new school year,' I said.

Hannah looked sceptical but she said she was not wholly against the idea. However, Paul, the other deputy present, looked completely unconvinced.

'Why does it need to be so rushed?' he asked. 'I think we are going to run into some real concerns from the staff that their subjects are being squeezed. I think a more gentle build-up might be easier to sell.'

I was convinced it was the right way forward and wasn't prepared to hang around while everyone discussed it and chipped away at what I already knew would be a tremendously effective initiative. Eager to move things on, I announced the changes at the next staff meeting. The staff listened in silence, but what was most unusual was there were no questions afterwards. I began to get an uneasy feeling and voiced my concerns to Peter Hyman when we got together for our regular meeting.

'I've glad you've raised this, because I was going to say

something,' he said. 'Lisa has already collared me and asked me to speak to you on her behalf. Her actual words were that you were "getting like Tony, floating off". She said, "The only person he now communicates with is his maker."'

I laughed at the comparison with Tony Blair, but it was obvious the situation was quite serious if the staff were asking Peter to intervene on their behalf. Most of them eyed him with suspicion and did their best to stay out of his way.

'There's a feeling you are running too far ahead of the rest of the staff with this Charter 7 thing,' Peter went on. 'I agree that it is a great idea, but you might want to think carefully about how you package it. People are scared about the pace of change.'

After that, things did begin to move quite quickly, although not necessarily in the way I wanted. A staff association meeting was called to discuss the plan and a number of concerns were raised. Staff spoke passionately about how they were worried their professionalism and conditions of service were being eroded. The changes to the curriculum needed to accommodate the new Year 7 timetable were a real stumbling block. The biggest problem by far, though, was the speed with which I wanted the changes to happen.

The staff took a vote on the motion: 'We, the staff of Islington Green School, feel that the Charter 7 idea should not be introduced in September 2004.' It was carried by twenty-six votes to two, with five abstentions.

I was pretty cross when I was told this and fired off an angry memo saying there would be a special briefing later in the week. When I cooled off, however, I thought about things more deeply. The idea itself was sound (as indeed was later proved); however, perhaps I had made a tactical error by trying to make it happen too quickly. Although I was convinced it was possible, I hadn't reckoned on how conservative the team would be and perhaps hadn't managed the proposal in the best way.

At the meeting later in the week, I said that I would delay the plan until September 2005 but assured the staff we would be making it happen and it would be a success. I was careful not to apologise for introducing the idea in the first place.

I said, 'The only thing I apologise for is our enthusiasm for a fantastic idea.

'We saw some of the best schools I have ever seen in the US. We are failing about 70 per cent of our kids and we must not allow ourselves to excuse this.'

To alleviate the tension, I added a jokey swipe at Tony Blair and his 'Iraq albatross': 'Unlike Peter Hyman's old boss, I can say, "Sorry I got this a bit wrong."'

Obviously a leader mustn't apologise too often, still less admit to making mistakes – only tactical errors. I may have over-estimated the teachers' enthusiasm by trying to make the changes too quickly, but I never wavered from my belief in the idea and indeed still believe it would have worked well if we had done it straight away. It wasn't so important though that I was prepared to jeopardise all the good will I had previously built with the team.

Chapter eleven

ACADEMY

In my first few years at Islington Green I oversaw dozens of projects to revamp the physical space of the school. We'd painted the place lilac from top to bottom, we'd modernised the IT suites, we'd set out on a rolling programme to install carpets and white boards in every classroom, we'd refurbished the canteen and performing-arts areas, and more. Each time we did anything, though, I was still acutely aware we were only ever fiddling around the edges. We were still no nearer to solving the fact that the building was completely unfit for purpose. It was difficult for the kids to get around, impossible to teach in and what's more the eyesore gave a never-ending negative impression to the community around us. Islington Green's grounds were totally exposed, which is never a good thing for a school whichever way you look at it. The only sensible thing to do was to raze it to the ground and start again.

It was a constant source of frustration that we were forever distracted by finding ways to shore up problems caused by the seven-storey building. The main hall, for example, was like an aircraft carrier. The ceiling went up three floors and had a big sloped roof. Apparently the original design intention had been to provide a good shape for top-notch acoustics, but that aim had most certainly not been achieved. I have a powerful voice, but it just disappeared in there. I'd be hoarse after each assembly. No wonder my predecessors relied on loudhailers. We installed a temporary lowered ceiling and some carpet tiles on the floor, but yet again we were just papering the cracks.

'When are you going to do something about it?' I was asked time and again by both staff and parents.

I wasn't short of ideas on how to redesign the place. The problem was, of course, the massive capital investment that would be needed. What was needed was a whole new, completely different layout. I had worked closely with our architect, Andy, to get plans drawn up. I'd based them on the traditional Essex design for schools made popular in the 1930s, which arranges school buildings around the perimeter of a central quad. It guarantees the school area is private and secure, which is vital in an inner-city location, plus adults get a good view of all the children while they are outside. The set-up also means it is easy for children to travel from one building to another, while gaining a little fresh air at the same time. We envisaged reducing the unmanageable seven storeys to two or three and arranging them in a U-shape around the existing site.

I'd been thinking about a potential rebuild from the moment I arrived at Islington Green, if not before, but raising enough money seemed an impossible task. One of the areas where I thought I might have some success was in the new breed of city academies championed by Tony Blair. Blair had established the idea of academies at the turn of the millennium and they were obviously his pet project. Indeed, schools were a big passion for Blair. As Peter Hyman explained to me, the Prime Minister was very keen to rebuild every school in the country so they could become a shining legacy of New Labour. David Miliband, the then Schools Minister, had already outlined an ambitious programme called Building Schools for the Future, promising that all secondary schools would be refurbished or replaced within the next fifteen years. This was, however, not soon enough for me. Islington Green needed urgent attention.

The idea of academies was still in its relative infancy as I joined Islington Green. At that stage the government was looking at a sponsorship arrangement where private-sector individuals or organisations contributed 10 per cent of academy costs, with the remaining £25 to £30 million coming from the government. Schools would be run independently from the local education authority and given considerably more freedom to innovate. The idea was to introduce a bit of private-sector best practice and innovative management to break the cycle of low performance. I explored the concept tentatively in 2003, but with so much on my plate elsewhere I didn't manage to get much traction behind it.

The following year, with Peter Hyman on board, I started to give it serious consideration. Right then it was just one of two options to get my much-needed cash injection to sort out the building. The first was David Miliband's Building Schools for the Future programme. Although I had been put off by the initially vague 'fifteen-year' time frame, CEA, a private company that had taken over the Islington Green local education authority, had submitted a bid to rebuild all of Islington's secondary schools. In my conversations with Penny, our link adviser at CEA, it appeared they seemed pretty confident of success.

It seemed to me they did indeed have a good chance of being awarded the money. Looking back at what had already been achieved by London Challenge, another Labour initiative, we already had ample examples of what good can be done with a minimum of effort. It wasn't a huge leap to imagine how we could transform the schools in the borough if they were given decent environments to operate in at long last.

Then, just as I was beginning to believe we were making progress at last, the shattering news came through. Islington was not going to be in the first wave of schools to receive funding. There was no clear reason why the money went to other London boroughs and elsewhere in the country and even Peter Hyman was unable to get a convincing explanation from his former paymasters. He was as gutted as I was and said he felt we were letting down the children at Islington Green, and we were.

Reeling from disappointment, I made a point of addressing parents directly via the school's newsletter. I said:

> You may have heard the PM and Secretary of State for Education announce on Tuesday their plan for the rebuilding of a number of schools in different authorities but excluding Islington. This is very sad news although Islington was invited to resubmit its bid for next year. In the meantime, I make a pledge to all members of Islington Green School community that I will strive to bring about the earliest confirmation of a rebuild. It is my view that our main building is in need of complete refurbishment or rebuild urgently. It is a weekly, sometimes daily, event that a major repair is required, drawing on much-needed funds and also disrupting the smooth running of the school.

It was time to explore option two: academy status. I asked Peter whether he could look into it for me, find out as much as he could from his old contacts at Westminster and report back. Right then there was an awful lot of rhetoric about 'beacons of excellence' that would 'provide real energy to the education system' but I wanted to know what it really meant. Peter spoke to Andrew Adonis in the Number Ten Policy Unit and Sir Bruce Liddington, a former head teacher who was now heading up the academies division of the Department for Children, Schools and Families. The view came back that it might be hard to present a convincing case for Islington Green because the academy system was targeting schools on their last legs. Schools with well under 25 per cent A* to C grades were the primary goal. Ironically, we had come too far and we were now considered to be a good school, on the up. Adonis did, however, say that there might be a possibility with a particular sponsor, a wealthy American who was looking to set up a foundation on these shores.

Peter went back to his old haunt at Number Ten to meet the man and returned with mixed messages. Ben, the would-be sponsor, undoubtedly had the money to spend. An ex-Goldman Sachs banker from New York, he now lived in London and had set up a charity called ARK Education, which had ambitious plans to sponsor a network of academies in the British capital. He was also pretty full-on, Peter explained.

'He is a man in a hurry,' Peter said, as he described the meeting. 'I'm used to pushy people, I mean I worked with Alastair Campbell for ten years, but this guy can be quite disconcerting. He constantly uses phrases like, "Don't give me excuses that we can't get there; tell me the way we can get there" and 'If you don't know, go find me someone who does." He constantly sounds frustrated that things are not moving quickly enough.'

'Sounds like an interesting guy to work with,' I said,

thinking he would be anything but. I couldn't imagine how my team would react to someone like this either. It had been hard enough to get them used to my ways and I seemed positively normal compared to the way Ben sounded.

'Well, I would be interested to see how you two get along,' Peter went on. 'You are either going to love him or hate him. Something you are going to have to accept though, Trevor, is that, if you go down the academy route, you will have less control. You'll be going into partnership with another body and having met Ben I don't ever see him being much of a silent partner.'

'I agree, but I can't see we have much choice. We should at least go ahead and meet him to see what he has to say.'

Peter had arranged for Ben to come into the school the following week to meet me and see whether he liked the set-up. I felt nervous and apprehensive but told myself at least we were moving in the right direction now.

The moment Ben and his entourage swept into Islington Green, I knew exactly what Peter had been trying to tell me. The man oozed confidence and self-satisfaction. He strode into my office like he owned the place, waving over at me as he continued to bark into his mobile phone. It took a supreme effort of self-control not to show him the door then and there.

When he finally turned to me, he spoke in exactly the way Peter had warned me.

'There are no excuses for not doing this right,' he said, speaking loudly and rapidly in the characteristic drawl of a New Yorker. 'We have our aims and we are going to do exactly what we set out to do. What I need to know today is if you are with us or not.'

I sensed it was easier to let his speech run its course and allow him to finish what I was sure was his usual set piece to subdue his opponents. As soon as I was able, I butted in to speak. I rapidly and confidently outlined where Islington Green was today, emphasising the great progress we had already made but adding how much more I felt we could do. I talked about the challenges we had with the building but also showed how we had overcome many other challenges with initiatives such as the Learning Zone and positive discipline. As I spoke, Ben nodded enthusiastically. Leaving aside his pushiness and impatience, this was clearly a very bright and engaged businessman. I could tell by the questions he asked that he'd understood what I was trying to do and was already on my wavelength.

After spending half an hour together in my office, Peter and I took Ben and his team on a tour of the school. The children were used to besuited visitors by now, after the succession of politicians and dignitaries who regularly visited the school. They barely even registered the group and were very well behaved too. When we arrived back in the office, Ben turned to me and stuck out his hand.

'We'll go for it,' he said, gripping my hand and shaking it firmly.

I couldn't quite believe what had just happened. Was it really going to be that easy?

Of course, it was never going to be that easy, as I very quickly discovered. Ben had very clear ideas of what he wanted and almost immediately set up another meeting, although this time he bought along Norman Atkins, a pioneering American educationalist. While they both spoke enthusiastically about lessons to be learned from the success of Charter schools, a great deal of which I agreed with and had even implemented at Islington Green, our thoughts did differ on some parts of the vision. Norman, for example, was passionate about what he called 'negative sell'. He believed that, if parents are told they shouldn't send their kids to a school if they didn't want to sign up to long hours, strict discipline and helping them with homework, they would queue up to join.

'I'm not sure long hours are the solution to the problem,' I said. 'My philosophy is it should be about the quality of the teaching, not the quantity. As for the negative sell, it's a great idea in theory, but you have to remember Charter schools operate on a significantly smaller intake. They are working with 100 kids; we cater for 1,050.'

I had to admit to myself, though, I enjoyed the debates with Ben and the various people he brought in to see me. In all my time in education, I had never yet been asked to articulate my philosophy in such a way and been questioned on it so rigorously.

By now, despite certain differences in outlook, I was warming to ARK and the academy concept. The SLT team seemed broadly supportive too. As Angela said when we debated the pros and cons, 'If you always do what you've always done, you'll always get what you've always got.'

To get rid of any lingering doubts, I decided to visit a few academies with Peter and the other members of the SLT. The first one, Bexleyheath Academy, was really impressive. It looked achingly modern, with open-plan classrooms, walkways leading to three floors, a high-tech canteen and an atrium with a podium for assemblies. The head had been very innovative with the timetable, switching to five terms a year with two weeks of holiday between each and four weeks over the summer. Students went off curriculum every Friday, working on projects with outside organisations, and lunch and break times were staggered.

The second academy we went to wasn't so impressive. Indeed, as we all subsequently agreed, it looked and felt a little prison-like. Morale among the teachers seemed really poor too and I was amazed that one of the teachers was openly critical of the school when we chatted. I'd always been fiercely loyal to Islington Green in public, whatever its faults, and yet this teacher seemed utterly prepared to talk her school down with a stranger she had only just met.

When I spoke to the head, the story was not encouraging either. He admitted it had been a difficult process becoming an academy, not least because the school had been heavily unionised. He hadn't wanted to include the unions in the new school plans and, he assured us, nor had the Department for Children, Schools and Families.

Many of the staff who had transferred to the new school were disillusioned and had even wanted to strike but were prevented from doing so by a High Court ruling that said they couldn't strike against a future employer.

We came away from our visits with mixed feelings but, on balance, still felt committed to the academy idea. The next step was to decide what we wanted for the school and to draw up a credible plan. Ben left me in no doubt that he expected something within days. No excuses.

The vision I mapped out centred on creating the impression of a smaller school, rather as we had done with our Charter 7 idea. It was, in some ways, inspired by the book *The Tipping Point* by Malcolm Gladwell, which says that units of 200 are the optimum size to create a meaningful community. I wanted to create a series of smaller schools, each with their own head, all reporting to one main principal. I had already seen the Year 7s benefit hugely from a more intimate atmosphere.

Working with Peter, I produced a vision paper that contained the following summary:

> When your child joins our Academy he or she will see a breath-taking modern school that is open-planned. A school that provides secure and open spaces to learn. A school organised with smaller schools inside it, so that every child is known to all their teachers.
>
> Our aim is that each child joining the school has a sense of awe and wonder while they are at the school. They will not only enjoy their

learning but love their school – feel it is part of their community, but one that challenges them with exciting new and inspiring experiences. A school that pledges to make learning active, personalised and demanding so that they progress as academics but also as people.

It was at this point that the wider Islington Green teaching community began to become aware of the plans afoot for the school. Ken Muller, the combative NUT rep, was not happy and immediately put a document in each teacher's pigeon hole with the headline 'Why the NUT, the *TES* and Professor Alan Smithers are All against (City) Academies.'

He included photocopies of a *TES* article questioning why 'property developers, holiday companies and car traders are able to govern schools better than representatives of the local community'. There was also a copy of the NUT resolution from its April annual conference opposing city academies. Documentary proof was also provided of Alan Smithers' robust assertions that the policy 'defies comprehension'.

The next salvo was to call a NUT meeting after school. Peter went along with Emma and Angela and when they reported back it sounded as though views were mixed. Some of the younger teachers spoke passionately against the idea, personally attacking Tony Blair for his modernising vision. Interestingly, the NUT regional rep who appeared had apparently given quite a balanced view of academies. Ken, whom I had asked to be on the project board overseeing the academy scheme, put up a strongly worded motion against the academy. However, when the vote was taken by a show of hands, only four voted in favour of the motion and five were against, with sixteen abstentions.

There was no room for complacency. I still had a job to do to convince my team and I still had to get the governors on board. Ahead of the governors' meeting, I circulated a memo to both governors and staff, along with a copy of the vision statement Peter and I had drawn up. I pledged not to break up the team of staff I had built up over the past two years and that no one would have to reapply for their job. There would be no increases in working hours and conditions of employment would remain the same. I emphasised that we were not working for Goldman Sachs and that ARK was not about to become the owner of the school. I finished by promising this was not a forerunner to selecting by ability but simply a way of getting the resources we needed to complete the job we had set out to do, which was in the best interests of all parties.

The meeting with the governors was tense. A number of them, most notably the Liberal Democrat counsellors and even a smattering of Labour representatives, were vehemently opposed to the idea, whatever form it took. I was curious about the stance that Bob, who was from CEA, the private company running the local education authority, would take. Bob and I got on well but he could be impatient and I suspected a little impulsive. He was a tall, well-built Scotsman who had always had quite a presence. He arrived late at the meeting and was visibly a little put out because the only chair left available was in the corner at the back of the room. Fortunately, though, when it was his time to speak, he rallied and seemed broadly in support of what we were trying to do.

The biggest thumbs up of all, though, came from Ces Darker, the chair of the governors. I had always got on well with Ces. She was a hugely flamboyant woman, tall, slim and attractive, and her best quality by far was that she was passionate about Islington Green. She had put her own kids through the school and even in its darkest hour had always truly believed in its potential.

'We all know what holds this school back. We've discussed the issues so many times and yet we now have an opportunity to do something,' she said to the assembled group. 'I understand the counter-arguments and why there might be reticence from some quarters, but we owe it to the children to see past them.

'We have to ask ourselves, if we don't do something now, when will we do something? More importantly, what will we do? We are running out of options and the upsides to this plan far outweigh the downsides in my view.'

Although her impassioned plea was met with support, we weren't out of the woods yet, and a number of people at the meeting still wanted to express grave reservations about ARK's intentions. Possibly one of the biggest stumbling blocks was the level of control the sponsor would get for its £2 million cash injection. As I had only just discovered, ARK would have the controlling vote on the governing body if everything went ahead. Many people were distinctly nervous of what might happen once control was handed over to this self-electing body.

'I can understand your concerns,' I said. 'It is something I have spent a lot of time talking about with the people from ARK. They have assured me they will only ever act in the best interests of the school and I personally believe their intentions are good. We've worked together on the vision for Islington Green and it wouldn't make any sense for ARK to suddenly veer off in an opposing direction. They want to work together with us on this.'

To my relief, at the end of the meeting, the group voted unanimously to push ahead with the idea.

It was a big step forward, but, as the weeks went on, my own feeling of discomfort about academies didn't go away. I couldn't escape the fact that my discussions with ARK had taken me a long way from my original vision, and the visit to the second academy, where the teacher had so obviously been unhappy about the new arrangement, niggled away at me. The team at Islington Green were united now and working together well, but it wouldn't take much to unsettle them. Ken Muller was already gaining a groundswell of support for his anti-academy stance.

My uncertainty wasn't helped by the fact Ben had all but disappeared from the scene, leaving his managing director, Delia, in charge. I never thought I would miss his constant heckling, challenges and demands, but, once I began working with Delia, I did. She didn't have any of her boss's charisma or persuasion. More importantly, she didn't have a background in education. She seemed to struggle with the idea of how the academy would work on a practical level. Every time I made a suggestion, she would reject it out of hand, which I was beginning to find extremely frustrating. Meanwhile, she doggedly stuck to Ben's 'no excuses' approach, even though she couldn't appear to make a decision on any suggestion.

I started to think that we really couldn't be an academy with these people.

The final straw was a consultation meeting with the local community, held in Islington Green's recently refurbished school library. It was Delia's idea to have the meeting, to lay out our stall and put to rest any niggling concerns once and for all. She invited teachers, union officials, governors and parents, many of whom had already signalled their strong opposition to the idea of an academy.

'I think it is a bad idea,' I said. 'It is a big crowd to manage and some of them will be quite hostile. If you are dead set on it, at least let me lead the meeting. I know all of them and we have a history.'

'I'm not going in there to make excuses, or to hide behind you,' she declared. 'I'll take the meeting.'

I tried a few more times to dissuade her, but she was a closed book.

In the end it was, just as I predicted, a disaster. The

people there tore shreds off Delia and didn't hold back in saying exactly what they thought. By the time she left the meeting, she looked utterly devastated. She clearly couldn't believe what had just happened.

I had had enough. The following day I called Bob at CEA to tell him the news. Islington Green was no longer pursuing city academy status, either with or without ARK. He wasn't particularly surprised. He'd been at the meeting and seen the reaction.

It was finally over. I felt shattered yet also strangely relieved. I had fully bought into the original idea, as discussed with Ben, but I hadn't been happy with the direction we had been going in for weeks. We were ending up a long way from my vision and if I couldn't give it my full support there was no chance of talking around all the people who were vehemently opposed to the idea.

As I prepared to leave the office to make my way home through the busy North London evening traffic, my mobile rang. I dug it out of my pocket and hit the reply button without really looking at who was calling.

'Trevor, it's Ben. I've just been brought up to speed with what has been happening. Listen, you can't go. We have to have you, Trevor. We love you, and Tony Blair and Peter think you're great. You can do it your way. It's all yours. You'll live by your results, though. What do you say?'

I hesitated. Five minutes ago I had been relieved I had walked away. Now I wasn't so sure. Everything had changed so quickly, I hadn't yet had a chance to think about how I would solve Islington Green's problems without the cash injection from academy status. The problems hadn't gone away just because the deal had.

Taking a deep breath, I was aware of a silence on the other end of the line. Ben was hardly ever silent. He was waiting for my response and, knowing him, I wasn't going to get a second chance.

'OK, we're in, but we do it my way,' I said, at last.

'Good call, Trevor, good call,' Ben boomed. 'Let's talk the details later.'

The phone clicked off and I was left staring at it. Islington Green was back in the game.

Flicking through my contacts list, I dialled Bob at CEA.

'Trevor?' By the sound of the background noise, Bob was at an airport.

'Yes, listen Bob, I've just been talking with Ben at ARK and Islington Green is back in. He's said we can do it our way this…'

I had hardly got to the end of my sentence before Bob exploded in a rage, apparently not caring as his deep Scottish accent resonated around the airport.

'Islington Green has been withdrawn from the process,' he shouted. 'I did it myself. It is not your school, Trevor. It is not your fucking school.'

Chapter twelve

FORCED OUT

My enthusiasm for being back in the game with ARK was short lived. Bob, who had made it very clear it was not my decision in our phone call, dug his heels in. As far as he was concerned, our discussions with ARK were closed and it was time to look at plan B.

His stance found a lot of support elsewhere. The choice of ARK to be our academy sponsor had never been popular among the staff, or indeed the community as a whole. Throughout the time we were in discussions, opponents to the whole idea of academies had whipped up a storm about the fact that ARK were a bunch of fat-cat bankers only interested in the bottom line. They had also highlighted the organisation's close links to Downing Street. Blair's chief of staff, Sally Morgan, had gone to work for ARK after leaving Downing Street, and his chief fundraiser, Lord Levy, had been instrumental in helping ARK auction a game of tennis with the Prime Minister at its charity dinner.

Ken Muller was quick to point out details such as the fact one of ARK's corporate sponsors was incorporated in the Cayman Islands and therefore out of the reach of the usual regulators. He was as vocal as ever and his comments fell on very willing ears. Few on the Islington Green teaching staff wanted academy status and, as far as the opposition were concerned, seeing off ARK would be a good step in the right direction. No opportunity was missed to publicly malign ARK and now the opposition had ARK's scalp.

Islington Green was back to square one. It was a bitter blow. I called a special staff meeting and told them that the academy scheme would still go ahead, one way or another.

I said, 'I know that a lot of you are opposed to the idea of academies on a political level but my job is not to be a politician, even though a lot of you think I am. My job is to get resources for the school and as many of them as I can get. You may all love the concrete, brutalist architecture of Islington Green but, let's be honest, this school is not fit for purpose.

'The best job I can do for all of you and for the school's future is to get the resources to knock this place down and rebuild it into a fantastic facility. If that means switching to another academy sponsor then we will. It will go ahead.'

Bob, who was just about to retire, went back to the Corporation of London, which had been one of our earlier options for sponsors, to see whether they would consider coming back on board. They said they would and a deal was put together whereby the Corporation offered £1 million and City University came in with a matching sum. City University, which is sited not far from Islington Green, said it wanted to cement its links with local secondary schools.

A glossy booklet called *Aiming Higher: City of London Academy Islington* was produced explaining the new academy would specialise in business and enterprise and be linked to financial services.

While the process marched relentlessly forward, I could not escape an overwhelming concern that I was no longer properly in control. My role in the academy process was unravelling. I had released a monster and it had taken on a life of its own. So many people had now chipped in, added their vision or taken away this, that or the other from the original one that it was nothing like what I had first envisioned. While I liked the idea of linking up with City University, I wasn't entirely convinced they were working with us for the right reasons. I sensed the entire project was being overtaken by a desire for power and influence rather than a desire to do what was best for Islington Green. Most worryingly, if I was not altogether convinced, how would I ever persuade the team to go forward with the plan?

It didn't help that I had other worries on my mind too. While all this was going on, I was wrangling with what to do about a huge budget deficit that had been discovered at Islington Green. It had taken some months to get to the bottom of the problem, which had begun to come to light when I joined the school. While I battled to cope with everything else that was going on, I couldn't help noticing the bursar still did the school budget on paper in a large lined book.

'How is it possible to accurately calculate a £7 million budget on paper?' I asked with genuine surprise. 'Why don't we have a computer for this?'

'It's fine, we've always done it like this,' he assured me.

There was that phrase again, I mused. It was a complete unwillingness to change that had always got the school into so much bother.

I didn't let it go and pushed hard for figures. Each week I would ask for new numbers on this or that and a few days later I would be furnished with the bare minimum. It was utterly exasperating. My unease wasn't helped by the fact people were regularly calling Islington Green to chase money. The school was clearly not paying its bills on time and that is never a good sign.

Finally, when the bursar was off sick, I seized my chance and brought in auditors.

'I want you to go through the books, get them online and tell me the exact position,' I instructed them.

Almost immediately, with very little investigation, they discovered a deficit of £275,000. It was devastating although not wholly unexpected news. My only option to get the budget back on track was to make some staff redundant, which was something I was really reluctant to do.

While I was still wrestling with what to do on the deficit, in the summer of 2006 the Islington council Overview Committee met to consider the latest academy proposal and after much debate the vote was split 4–4. It went through on the chair's casting vote. At long last it looked as though I might be leading the rebuilding of Islington Green with the much-needed cash injection.

Now the votes had been cast I was finally able to concentrate on making concrete plans for the future and began working hard to build and motivate the team that would help me realise my vision for a successful academy. The school was already earning a solid reputation and, even though most of the staff were still opposed to the idea of becoming an academy, everyone was buoyed by the fact the school was so clearly on the up.

I told the staff about the budget deficit and announced there would be some redundancies among the senior team, but on a voluntary basis only. I added that we would be bringing in a number of new staff lower down the ranks, so we would still be strong going forward. Both Emma and Angela elected to leave. Emma took voluntary redundancy along with her partner Marek. They decided to take a year off and travel around India. Angela, who had been teaching for twenty years, opted to retire. I was really sorry to see them go because they had both been an essential part of the SLT team. We'd been through so much together and they had made a vital contribution, but I was fully supportive of their wish to move on.

One of the most obvious signs of the new sense of

optimism around the school came whenever we recruited new members of staff. When I first applied for the headship, there had been just two other applicants. Now, we routinely received dozens of applicants for each post we advertised. They were high-quality ones too. Indeed, when we advertised in the spring of 2006, we got 120 applications for one post and I noticed with satisfaction that we were getting CVs from Oxbridge-educated teachers. This was a first for Islington Green. Finally we were getting the pick of the best, and deservedly so.

Of course, the higher calibre of candidates came with its challenges too. Many of the new recruits were sticklers for process, which was something I wasn't entirely used to. This was something I particularly found to be the case with Tim, one of the new members of staff. He was clearly uncomfortable with the way I ran things.

'I was wondering if you have my job description,' he said, on his first day.

'I don't really believe in job descriptions,' I said, watching his eyes widen in shock. 'If I write down that you are in charge of the mailing list and then one day there is nothing to do on the mailing list, I want you to use your initiative and do other stuff.'

Tim very obviously didn't like this approach, but it didn't stop him hanging around my door at every opportunity to ask why we didn't have processes for this, that and the other. He wanted timelines for this, accountabilities for that. The more he wanted to be serious, the less I wanted to be. To be honest, it started to drive me just a little bit mad and I could see my reaction was driving him crazy too.

Of course, what I should have realised was that he would find others among the team who were willing to listen to his criticisms. While the teachers had been very supportive of what I had done in the school, there was still a huge undercurrent of unrest about the whole idea of the academy. The closer we got to realising it, the more uncomfortable people felt.

Then, as we were nearing the end of the summer term of 2006, it all came to a head. Eleanor, who had taken over Bob's role at CEA following his retirement, called me to say she needed to see me urgently. I went straight over to her office. When I was shown to her room I could tell straight away it was serious. She had a grave expression on her face and didn't say a word as she pushed an A4 brown envelope across the desk.

'What is that?' I asked. 'Are you finally giving me my cards?'

Eleanor wasn't in the mood for my jokes and my words hung in the air, foolish and unacknowledged.

'You'd better take a look.'

I took the envelope and reached inside it. Pulling out a bundle of A4 papers, I glanced at the first page. It was a letter to Eleanor, with the subject heading 'Concerns about the professionalism of Islington Green headmaster Trevor Averre-Beeson'.

'It's a dossier that makes a number of allegations against your leadership of the school,' Eleanor said flatly.

My senses were reeling. For a few moments it felt like the world around me was in fast forward while I was motionless in the middle of it all.

'Who?' I said it with some difficulty because my mouth felt so dry.

Eleanor nodded at the signatures at the bottom.

'The letter has numerous signatories on the staff. It looks like a number of people have contributed to the report.'

I looked at the bottom of the letter, but it was hard to focus. The letters swam in front of my eyes as I struggled to take it all in. My relationship with some of the team had not been as good as I would have hoped, but I thought we'd found a way to work together. Some of the names were from new recruits such as Tim, but there were signatures from a number of people who had been at the school for a little while. I was relieved that signatures such as Peter's, Angela's and Emma's weren't there, but there were a few from the senior and middle tiers of the team, including Hannah's. It felt like a real kick in the teeth because I had thought they were fully on board.

'I think you need to take some time to read it and then maybe we should chat again?' Eleanor said. Her voice was softer and more gentle than usual. She could see this was a huge shock.

'OK,' I said, sliding the papers back into their envelope. 'Thank you.'

After I left the office I went straight back to school.

I didn't read the dossier straight away. I couldn't bring myself to even take it out of its innocent-looking brown envelope. I stayed in my office for the rest of the day. I didn't have the strength to face my accusers and right then I didn't even know who they all were.

I left at the end of the school day, taking the envelope with me. It wasn't until late in the evening that I finally opened it again and drew out the dossier.

It made chilling reading. Everything I had done over the past four years was put under the microscope in both my private and professional lives. By far the biggest opprobrium was reserved for my relationship with head of year Jane Fielding. Jane was the cheeky teacher who had confronted me in the staff room when I first joined and we had grown close over time. I'd chosen her to show Peter Hyman the ropes and we had started a relationship in February 2005 at the launch party of his book *1 out of 10: From Downing Street to Classroom Reality*, which chronicled his time at Islington Green. Neither Jane nor I tried to hide the relationship and I had openly announced to the entire school we were to be married. We had both been single before we got together. Indeed, I had been divorced from my first wife some years earlier. However, the dossier inferred I was somehow giving Jane special treatment thanks to our relationship.

Some of the allegations were risible. They said, for example, I had closed the school for a day so I could take Jane for a spa trip. In actual fact, on the date in question, the police had advised me to close the school because

Arsenal had won the FA Cup and were holding a victory parade through the streets of Islington. Thanks to our location smack bang in the middle of the borough, the authorities felt it was the safest option for all concerned if the kids weren't in school, so I complied. I was with Jane that day, but the dossier completely twisted the facts.

Another of the supposedly incriminating pieces of evidence was that I had allegedly allotted Jane a spot in the senior leaders' car park. This was completely ridiculous, not least because there was no senior leaders' car park. I used the same parking space every day, and occasionally if we came into school together in Jane car she would leave it in my space. There was certainly no sort of 'them and us' preferential treatment.

Most upsetting was the accusation that I had created an impenetrable inner circle around me. Teachers apparently felt that they were either 'in' or 'out' and the supposed outsiders were deeply resentful of this implied slight. This came as a huge surprise to me because I thought I had carried everyone with me on the journey. I had never been one to say, 'I don't like him or her, so they are out.' I had a fair few really awkward whatnots on the team too.

My detractors also felt I was overly interested in behavioural management and relationships rather than academic rigour. I found this quite distressing. As a former teacher I was very focussed on the learning side; however, at the same time I was always aware that if we didn't sort out the behavioural issues our teaching would be the equivalent of fighting with one arm tied behind our backs.

The issue of the budget deficit was raised in the context that I had somehow frittered away the money on frivolous projects. It was as though I had personally created this massive over-spend, and the accusations neatly ignored the fact I had been the one who unravelled the archaic accounting system that had caused the real problem.

Reading on, I saw I had even been criticised for announcing my engagement to Jane in the school bulletin. According to my detractors, this symbolised my paternalistic approach. I had simply put it there because our relationship was now public knowledge and I had wanted to thank everyone for their good wishes.

As I worked my way through the dossier, my heart sank. I realised everything I had done for the past six months had been watched, picked over and criticised by a team of people who wanted nothing more than to get me out. Interestingly, virtually none of the naysayers had been there right from the beginning. They hadn't been by my side on the journey to take the school out of serious weaknesses and turn it into one of the best performing secondary schools in the borough.

My dogged support of the academy process had sealed my fate. While everyone around me couldn't fail to see what I had helped them achieve, the change of status was deeply unpopular.

I spent many hours reading and rereading the dossier. I kept swinging between an overwhelming feeling of helplessness and one of sheer blinding rage. I just couldn't see how I was supposed to deal with the betrayal. I had absolutely no idea what to do next. To make my decision even harder, I was acutely aware that, in a matter of weeks, both Angela and Emma would be leaving the school. (Even this was criticised in the dossier, which claimed I was 'paying off' my close pals, again neatly ignoring the reality that I had little choice following the deficit.) There would be no one there to watch my back. I would be permanently exposed to the people who had produced the dossier.

I couldn't help but question myself. Had I been too hubristic? Had I been so carried away by the vision of what we could achieve, indeed were achieving, that I stopped looking behind me?

The following day, exhausted from a largely sleepless night, I met with Eleanor and Ces, the head of the school governors.

'There is no way I can do my job in an atmosphere where every move I make is being noted down and criticised in this underhand way,' I began. 'The people who have done this should at the very least face disciplinary action.'

'Let's not be too hasty,' said Eleanor, flapping her hands up and down as though she was damping down a fire. 'I know the way they have gone about it is a bit underhand…'

'A bit underhand?' I was incredulous.

'…but we need to look at the bigger picture,' Eleanor ploughed on. 'They obviously feel pretty strongly about this, or they wouldn't have gone to all this trouble. I think it would be more constructive to talk about how we can bring them alongside you so you can work together effectively.'

I could hardly believe what I was hearing.

'Yes, bring them into the tent, as they say,' agreed Ces.

'But a lot of the stuff in there is factually wrong,' I began.

'We need to find a way to get over that and move on,' Eleanor said as Ces continued to nod away.

So that was it. I had no support from the senior team around me. They had told me I had to deal with the situation, so I didn't have much choice. However, I couldn't let it just pass by without comment. When I got back to the school following my meeting with Eleanor and Ces, I called three of the worst perpetrators into my office one at a time. I told each one that if they ever did anything like this again they would face a full disciplinary warning. It gave me no satisfaction though and I already knew things wouldn't be the same.

Things limped along for a few days, but the atmosphere among the SLT was clearly strained. Our meetings were stilted and perfunctory. Luckily we were all working flat out on the usual end-of-term shenanigans but I was relieved when the school finally broke up for the summer. I had never felt so exhausted in my life.

Obviously the situation couldn't continue. There was no way we would all come back in September and suddenly start behaving like nothing had happened. We had gone way beyond that. I needed a plan.

Hugh Richie was the obvious sounding board. He had

always been around in the background, ever since my first headship at Mayfield, and consistently gave me sage and well-considered advice.

'Can you come and do a management review and help me formulate a plan on how we might move forward in September?' I asked him, after outlining the situation to date.

A few days later, he came to see me at my home in Chelmsford. He was clutching a large brown envelope and I couldn't stop my mind flashing back to the dossier.

He put the report, unopened, on the table between us.

'I can give you the report or I can give you the headline advice in one sentence,' he said, looking at me steadily. 'You choose.'

I paused and looked at Hugh, weighing up what he had just said.

'OK, the headline advice,' I nodded. 'Let's have that.'

'You need to get out of there. Go now, before you are chased out.'

For a few moments I could hardly believe what he was saying. Leave Islington Green, just when I was on the verge of getting the investment I had pursued for so long? Get up and go in response to a report that wasn't just blatantly unfair but also riddled with factual inaccuracies?

It was as though Hugh could read my thoughts.

'It doesn't matter that they are wrong. You can't sack them and there is no way they will take the threat of disciplinary action lying down. They will just keep going until they get you sacked.'

I nodded as the awfulness of what faced me began to sink in. I had been so excited about leading the new academy.

'We had come so far,' I said, for a moment thinking back to my first day at Islington Green and the madness I had found there.

'Go and get married and leave while the going is good. It's the only choice you have.'

Resigning was, without a doubt, the toughest career decision I have ever faced. I really had no idea of how to go about telling the team I was leaving. Although I already knew some of them would be delighted, I knew many would see it as a real blow. They believed in me and they believed in the journey we'd taken together. They were not going to understand why I had bailed out before we reached the finishing line.

In an entirely unconnected move I had applied some months earlier to take a leadership course with the National College for School Leadership, and I wondered whether this might offer a credible reason for my departure. I had applied before the dossier blew up and had spoken about the course with the governors. It would have involved being out of the school for four days a week for a few months. The governors had been reluctant at the time but agreed, and we talked about Angela covering for me while I was on the course. It seemed to me now that this was the perfect get-out.

In the second week of the autumn term, I called all the staff together and told them I would be leaving the school at half term to go on the leadership course and I would not be returning after that. I found it hard to deliver the message in a steady voice and seeing the shock begin to register on the faces of some of my colleagues made it even harder to keep my composure.

My reasons for opting to do the course were kept deliberately vague, but everyone knew something significant was up. It is highly unusual for a head to leave halfway through a school term. We are expected to serve out a full term to give the school time to find a replacement and to ensure a good handover. Of course, with any vague story like this, people will always rush to fill the news vacuum and the conspiracy theorists had a field day.

According to industry gossip, I didn't jump, I was pushed out by Downing Street. It was a theory I didn't really understand because I had always had good links with Westminster, not least through Peter. *The Guardian* called and asked straight out what the truth was, but I was unwilling to say right then because it was all too raw so they made up their own minds. According to the article they wrote, I was pushed out because I had lost enthusiasm for the academy project.

In a cruel twist, the National College for School Leadership called me to withdraw the offer of a place on the heads' leadership course because I was no longer a serving head. So, having told everyone that the course was what I was going off to do and with it having appeared in the press, this now made my exit messier than ever. It was a real low point.

Even as I kept my head down and served out my last few weeks, I saw things at Islington Green really begin to unravel. CEA announced that the school's remaining £260,000 deficit, which was to be paid off over several years, now had to be paid off *before* the school switched to academy status. It became clear that at least a further fourteen teachers would have to be made redundant so the money could be repaid. If the staff were unsure about the academy idea before, this ensured they were downright hostile to it now.

Meanwhile, Edison, a large American firm, emerged as a front-runner to sponsor the academy. Staff and parents were even more alarmed at this prospect. Edison had pioneered a strategy that offered impoverished schools free use of a satellite receiver, videos, TVs and a PA system. In return pupils were required to watch a ten-minute current-affairs broadcast each day, with two minutes of advertising in the middle from blue-chip giants such as Pepsi, Reebok, Twix and Clearasil.

In October, shortly before I left, Ken Muller organised a staff ballot in which 94.7 per cent of the 78 per cent turnout said they did not agree with the school becoming an academy. The poll results were sent to local councillors, urging them to change their minds. Ironically, since Ken had opposed so many of my initiatives, he cited the school's significant improvements in GCSEs and SATs as evidence the idea of an academy was flawed.

The arguments rumbled on as I prepared to leave, although now I felt strangely remote from them all. It transpired that I was not to be replaced by a permanent head, in the light of the probability the school would be changing status shortly. On 31 October, my last day at Islington Green, I had a heavy heart. I had an overwhelming sense that I had not done all I had set out to do and it was deeply frustrating not to be able to lead the school through the difficult times ahead towards what I still believed could be a bright, exciting future.

As I walked away from my office that day, it was hard to accept it was all over. I took one last, nostalgic walk around outside, glancing up ruefully at the seven-storey building I had not managed to rebuild. I passed Matthew, a Year 10, sitting alone on a bench, as was his way. I liked Matthew. He was autistic and never comfortable around other kids, but he did get on well with adults. I'd often stopped to speak to him on my rounds. He was a huge fan of *Hancock's Half Hour* and liked nothing more than to repeat back a sketch, virtually verbatim.

'I hear you are leaving, sir,' he said, looking up as I walked past.

'I am,' I replied. Even as I said it, I still couldn't believe it.

'I don't blame you sir.'

'That is kind of you Matthew. Why do you say that, though?'

'Well, they're a right lot to have to deal with, aren't they?'

'Oh, they're not that bad, you know. I know a lot of the children can be quite difficult to deal with sometimes and you don't always get on with them, but most of them are really nice and I'm very sorry to be leaving them.'

'I wasn't talking about the children, sir. I was talking about the teachers. You've got some really difficult characters there haven't you.'

I laughed, despite myself. Matthew had it about right.

AFTERWORD

A lot was undone at Islington Green after I left. The school still hadn't quite become an academy and the interim head used his own judgement on what needed to be done at the school. Who knows how highly influenced he was by the staff, who apparently wanted to get back to the old regime of excluding as many kids as possible. When I was there I saw there were certainly many on the team who still struggled to agree with a system that recognised the good in anyone. Perhaps it was because it involved them having to work harder. Either way, the system of positive discipline was immediately ditched. A number of the people who I had promoted because I felt they had real talent were moved on or demoted. In a short space of time, everything began to fall apart. Ironically, it all had the effect of making Islington Green an even more perfect candidate for academy status, because the system was originally intended for failing schools.

Controversy about the school never really went away after that. In early 2008, Ken Muller used a freedom of information request to dig into the 1997 Ofsted decision. Much of the paperwork had been destroyed, but there was a memo dated November 1997 from HMI Barry Jones to the then chief inspector Chris Woodhead stating that the Ofsted team had disagreed with the judgement, adding they were 'of the unanimous view that the school was not failing'. A handwritten note from Chris Woodhead at the top of the memo said Liz Passmore, Ofsted's then Head of School Improvement, would explain the decision to Barry Jones when she saw him. No information has ever been forthcoming on the substance of the explanation. Ken Muller has demanded an apology and a retrospective overturning of the decision but the official line remains that the decision was 'properly made'.

My own view, for what it is worth, is the school did undoubtedly warrant special measures. It had notoriously gone through cycles of success and failure and it didn't help that the teaching staff and leadership team approached Ofsted like the enemy. I suspect, although I don't know for certain, that during the crucial inspections the team thought they would teach Ofsted a lesson, showing how difficult the school was and how well they were coping given the circumstances. They certainly set the inspectors up next door to the behavioural unit and, perhaps predictably, the first thing that happened was one of the children burst in and shouted, 'Who the fuck are you?'

Right then, Ofsted wasn't particularly sophisticated in analysing children's academic progress and, while the progress was possibly 'good', the school was quite clearly out of control. There were hundreds of exclusions and the teachers took more notice of the NUT rep than of the head. The leadership wasn't in control and the governance wasn't either. That is why it went into special measures.

For my part, I initially went to work for the American company Edison, whose management had offered me a job the moment they heard I was leaving Islington Green. They wanted me to put together a bid to run Salisbury School, which I did, and we duly won the contract. It was another school that had been in special measures, with hundreds of exclusions and just 9 per cent A* to C grades. My old Islington Green deputy, Angela, came out of retirement to help me there, as well as the assistant head Jessica, and the three of us went to Salisbury for what was to be a three-year contract. At the end of the last year, at which point we had got Salisbury up to 27 per cent A* to C grades (it rose to 37 per cent the following year), Edison asked me to begin to prepare a bid for the next school. That was when I had a light-bulb moment and thought: why do I want to do this for other people? I would be far better off running my own company. After all, I already knew the ropes about making a bid and I certainly knew all about how to run a failing school.

In 2009, Lilac Sky Schools began business and many of my old Islington Green colleagues now work with me, including Emma, Angela and of course my wife, Jane. At the time of writing, we have run fourteen schools under contract and are sponsors of ten academies. We employ more than 470 people and have gone from a turnover of £150,000 in the first year to one in excess of £10 million.

My involvement with the corridors of power in

Westminster is nowhere near as intense as it was during my period at Islington Green, but as time has gone on I have developed good links with those who decide on education policy. I've even been called upon to give my views now and again, which is immensely satisfying.

For example, I got to meet Michael Gove, the former Secretary of State for Education. I invited him to open the school in Enfield in 2008, when he was Shadow Secretary of State for Children, Schools and Families. Gove subsequently invited me to speak at an event in London and then to join an education forum he was setting up. The forum, which was held at the House of Commons, was essentially a gathering of around 100 educators who were invited to hear about some of the policies Gove would be introducing in the coming months. Half a dozen of those educators were subsequently asked for one-to-one meetings with Gove and his then deputy, Nick Gibb. I was one of them.

I was quite excited about the prospect. The way I saw it, I had an hour to potentially influence future education policy. It is quite rare to be given an opportunity like that and I needed to use it wisely. In the run up to the event, I gathered together a group of some of my most trusted and intellectual educational colleagues to canvas their views.

'What do you think we can do that will make a difference?' I asked them.

After much discussion, we came up with three ideas that we thought would have a real impact. Top of the list was to make a real, meaningful investment in training and coaching teachers. Typically, most schools set aside £10,000 or £20,000 of their budget each year for training and then charge a fairly lowly member of staff with the responsibility to organise something. They will set up one training day a year, maybe two, or a couple of half days, all on a very ad hoc basis. In absolute truth, though, 99 times out of 100, the training is a jolly. Everyone will troop off to London and listen to someone talking about how to deal with difficult children for a short while before dispersing for an afternoon in the capital with their bulging goody bag. They'll return to school and then carry on exactly as they have done before. It is not really training.

If pilots were trained like that there would be a lot more crashes. It is like someone saying, 'There are a range of ways in which you might like to fly your plane and here are two or three we would recommend. We will tell you about them in one day and then you can go off and fly your plane for the rest of the year.' If that was what really happened, no one would ever risk flying ever again.

Inset days, which were introduced more than twenty-five years ago to resolve the training problem, have never properly worked. They were the brainchild of Mrs Thatcher's fearsome Education Secretary, Ken Baker, and, as most teachers of a certain age will remember, he had to push hard to get the idea through because the days came out of school holidays. Eventually, the pill was sugared with a 25 per cent pay rise, but insets were never used properly and are even less so today. Inset days are still referred to by older staff as 'Baker days'. Teachers always wear casual clothes on inset days, which is a tradition that began as a mild protest because the days were taken from the summer holiday. It is childish and irritating behaviour although younger staff probably don't know the historical origin.

The pattern is familiar at every school I've joined, both as a head and as the sponsor through Lilac Sky. One or two of the five insets always fall at the beginning of the autumn term. Teachers have been away from school for the six long weeks of summer and rely on insets as a time to organise the classroom, put up new posters and generally clear the decks. OK, these are necessary activities but, let's be honest here, they are essentially fiddling around. I know exactly what happens. I am always sure to have a session with teachers at both the beginning and end of the day, just to make sure they stay in school. Otherwise I can never be sure they will even hang around for the whole inset. I start the day with coffee and croissants, let them know how marvellous the end-of-year results were and then let them go off and have time in their departments. Then I bring them together at the end of the day and tell them some things I would like them to focus on for the coming term.

Training-wise, though, it is hardly cutting-edge stuff. There is a lot of room for improvement. My suggestion to Michael Gove was to do something to formalise training rather than leaving it in the rather vague situation we have endured for many years.

But how could I present this idea? John Bayley, a well-known behaviour expert and education consultant, suggested that one way to appeal to the minister might be to draw an analogy with another profession that has a reputation for strong training.

'He's a Tory, isn't he, so it will appeal to him if you talk to about how well doctors are trained,' suggested John.

Thinking about the model where hospitals act as training theatres for doctors sparked the idea that schools could follow the same model. What if a school could be given training-school status and become an arena where teachers could be given on-the-job training by respected professionals? The hands-on element would certainly be a lot more relevant than a remote, academic-based training programme at a university and would cater for a wider range of teachers, not just the ones straight out of education.

When I outlined the idea to Michael Gove he nodded and said it was very helpful. Since then, the government has introduced a system where outstanding schools in each local authority can bid to become a training school, and I believe it is a policy that is working very effectively. It may, or may not, be a direct result of my recommendation that day, but I like to think that I have done something to have a positive influence on developments in teacher training. It is certainly long overdue.

Something along the same vein that we have already

introduced at Lilac Sky is an Outstanding Teacher Diploma, which puts our best teachers and deputies together with an underperforming teacher for ten weeks. They are not together every day. They might interact for only a couple of hours a week, either supporting the teacher in a lesson or before or after a lesson. The mentor comes with a big folder of published materials that have been collaboratively put together. It contains a lot of helpful ideas about good teaching practice and guidance for the teacher on attaining quick, practical wins. The outcomes have been quite remarkable, with 90 per cent of teachers moving up an Ofsted grade in the ten-week period.

To be honest, I was surprised how well the Outstanding Teacher Diploma system works. At first I questioned whether the outstanding results were a fluke. Perhaps we just had a genius coach on board, or had got lucky. Yet, we got similar results time after time. Today we guarantee that 75 per cent of teachers who sign up to the Outstanding Teacher Diploma will go up an Ofsted grade in ten weeks. The caveat is, it obviously won't work for teachers who are constantly off work or clearly incapable. However, with any bog standard teacher who is on the verge of being satisfactory, or is even less than satisfactory, we will get them up to being regularly good.

The reason the model works so well is the very same reason the London Challenge was so effective. If you do nothing to train or coach teachers for years and years, guess what: they won't improve. Yet, if you put in place a meaningful training programme, you will see a transformation.

There are many other ways to transform our schools and it is my vision to continue to do that in the schools I work with. However, I would also like to see the benefits of my experience used elsewhere. It is for this reason I close this book with my own manifesto on the most effective ways to achieve almost instant, measureable results.

The Lilac Sky Manifesto

1. Firstly, I would like to see an end to the current trend for a football-management style in hiring and firing heads. We need to find a way to promote and sustain longer-term leadership for the stability and growth of our schools. I believe the best way to do this is to take a more team-orientated approach where there will be a number of people in leadership positions within a school. This does not mean that there would not be a central person in charge, but rather that there would be a number of associate heads who would work together towards a common aim.

2. There is, as I discovered at Islington Green and again found at Lilac Sky, an urgent need for a structured programme of continuous coaching for teachers. It should be properly resourced and supported at every level. I fully support the idea

of training schools introduced by Michael Gove and hope the scheme won't be quietly dropped because it no longer suits the political will of the day.

3. In particular, there needs to be intensive retraining to change the culture that has become prevalent in so many of our schools, so that teachers understand that sarcasm, hostility and aggression are a demoralising and degrading way of managing children. Positive intelligent discipline needs to be the norm. We have to learn the lessons from psychology about positive recognition. Every adult knows positive recognition is valid, yet in the vast majority of schools you won't find it being exercised.

4. The issue of governance is now being looked at seriously, thanks to recent news events, and that is long overdue. Once again, my wish is that this issue does not become hijacked by political posturing and that something positive comes out of it. At the very least, I would want to see all governors educated to degree level. Teaching is a sophisticated post-graduate profession; it is ludicrous that not all governors are graduates.

5. Finally, there is an urgent need to address education for children with special needs. I have

long been appalled about how little is done in this respect. The funding available is dreadful, yet this is the most vulnerable group of youngsters in our society. It is a sign of a good society when the most vulnerable are looked after, yet we fall a long way short. These children deserve the best teachers, the best resources and the best school environments money can buy, yet right now they receive the opposite.

Many of these points were learned during my time at Islington Green. It was an enormous privilege to work there and also a hugely frustrating, exhausting and all-consuming period. With the passage of time I can look back on what I achieved in a positive way and if anyone asks whether I have any regrets about that time, I always answer in the same way.

Only one: that I didn't take the Pink Floyd discs with me when I left. At some point during the numerous changes of senior staff that occurred in the following years, the discs vanished. No one knows where they have gone and a little slice of history has disappeared. Looking on this in a positive way, as I am apt to do, it was an honour and privilege to have them around me while it lasted. We had fun.